DELIVERANCE AND INNER HEALING

THE MINISTRY
OF JESUS AND THE BELIEVER

EDGAR A. IRAHETA

Edgar A. Iraheta | permission@edgarandvictoria.org
177 Apostles Way, Box A, Santa Rosa Beach, Fl 32450.
http://www.edgarandvictoria.org

Cover Design by Pixelstudios at Fiverr.com

PRINT ISBN: 978-0-9991302-0-9

For eBook version visit: books.pronoun.com/edgariraheta/

First Edition: June 2017

10 9 8 7 6 5 4 3 2 1

Contents

FOREWORD

BY APOSTLE SHARON PARKES

The Ministry of deliverance brings much con-
troversy in the church today. Even though
scripturally we know this was a vital ministry of Jesus. Whether because of fear or ignorance
on the subject most ministries do not offer this in
their Churches.

"And these signs shall follow them that believe; In
my name shall they cast out devils-they shall speak
with new tongues." (Mark 16:17 KJV) This scripture
alone should be enough to validate the ministry of
deliverance. But I believe it's a tactic of the enemy
to get into theology and say it is not for today and not
necessary.

My husband and I launched the Deliverance Ministry at Christian International almost 20 years ago.
We have seen thousands set free and have trained

others in many nations to set the captives free. And it still amazes me how many churches have closed the door on deliverance ministry.

Edgar has conducted an extensive research on deliverance and inner healing from other ministries but also the scriptural basis of why this ministry is so important to the body of Christ. He also shares from his heart his personal experience in this area.

In this book, he addresses the question about deliverance and inner healing and backs it up with the word of God. I have known Edgar for the 10 years that he's been here at Christian international and endorse this book. I know you will get revelation as you read it and keys to set you free.

Apostle Sharon Parkes, *Director of Healing and Deliverance at Christian International and Author of : Passport to Freedom, Breaking the Cycle of Abuse and Prophetic Healing and Deliverance*

SPECIAL THANK YOU

A special thank you to my wife, Victoria, for your sacrificial support in the process of writing this book. Without you I would not have been able to write this empowering message that will bring freedom to countless lives. I love you!

I also want to give a special thank you to my friend, Pastor Ned Maraman. You kept encouraging me to put this teachings into a book. You even gave me the opportunity to exercise this revelation and ministry, for that I am thankful!

A LONG BUT IMPORTANT ONE

"Nearly two thousand years ago Jesus came to the help of suffering humanity, working miracles by healing the sick and casting out demons. Throughout the three and a half years of His earthly ministry, this never changed.

In the intervening centuries Christian men and women have been called from time to time with miraculous ministries to the sick and afflicted. Yet, as far as I know, there are few, if any, records of people with a ministry of casting out demons comparable to that of Jesus'. As a result, most victims of demonic oppression have been left to suffer without any offer of practical help from the Church. The time has come, I believe, to clear away the rubble of religious tradition that has obscured the clear revelation of the New Testament, and to reestablish the Church's ministry on the bedrock of Jesus and the gospels."

Derek Prince

They Shall Expel Demons: What You Need to Know about Demons— Your Invisible Enemies

This is a long but important introduction to this book. This introduction lays the foundational framework that is necessary for you to understand and apply the rest of this book. Let's get started...

> Matthew 10:1 And he called to him his twelve disciples and gave them authority over unclean spirits, to cast them out, and to heal every disease and every affliction.

> Matthew 10:7-8 And proclaim as you go, saying, 'The kingdom of heaven is at hand.' Heal the sick, raise the dead, cleanse lepers, cast out demons. You received without paying; give without pay.

> 1 John 3:8 The reason the Son of God appeared was to destroy the works of the devil.

> Colossians 2:15 He disarmed the rulers and authorities and put them to open shame, by triumphing over them in him.

As I read these scriptures, I heard God say, *"Many are oppressed because my Church decided to abdicate the authority I have given to them."* We cannot accomplish our mandate without challenging Satan's rule.

I looked up the definition of *"abdicate,"* and it means: to renounce or relinquish a throne, right, power, claim, responsibility, to give up or renounce (authority, duties, an office, etc.)

When I read this, all I could pray was *"Lord, forgive us; we repent!"* Jesus has made every tool, weapon, resource and provision available to us to live a victorious life. It's up to us to believe and allow Him to work in and through our lives. Have you abdicated your authority? Have you relinquished the throne God has given you? Have you given up the power given to you through the Holy Spirit? How about the responsibility to give freely as you have received?

THE AUTHORITY

Matthew 10:1 says that He "gave them authority." It means it was entrusted to them, to be stewards of the authority and power obtained through the suffering, death, and resurrection of Jesus on the Cross. The word authority here is exousia it means the power, right, and authority to give commands, the power of one whose will and commands must be obeyed by others in this case we have been given authority so that unclean spirits, disease, and every affliction obey our command.

Jesus has given us the authority to exercise power over the works of the enemy. When we do not use it, we abdicate that authority. It's our lawful authority because we are God's sons and daughters.

When Father God gives you keys, you can use them or not, and it's up to you. When we don't use them, we wonder if Father God forgot us. The truth is, He never did. He equipped us, and we just abdicated the keys back to Him.

THE RESPONSIBILITY

Matthew 10:7-8 says,

"And proclaim as you go, saying, 'The kingdom of heaven is at hand.' Heal the sick, raise the dead, cleanse lepers, cast out demons. You received without paying; give without pay."

Jesus gave responsibility to His disciples. They were to proclaim that, *"The kingdom of heaven is at hand."* To demonstrate the Kingdom through the healing of the sick, raising the dead, cleansing the lepers and casting out demons. But more than anything to give as you have received, *"freely."*

THE REASON

John 3:8 says,

> "The reason the Son of God appeared was to destroy the works of the devil."

Other translations say, *"For this purpose,"* in other words, if you need a reason or purpose to exercise your spiritual authority, you have one here: to destroy the works of the devil.

We must understand, there is no greater reason or purpose to exercise our God-given Spiritual Authority than to destroy the works of the Devil. It is a responsibility we have and must fulfill as Jesus did.

THE VICTORY

Colossians 2:13-15 says,

> "And you, who were dead in your trespasses and the uncircumcision of your flesh, God made alive together with him, having forgiven us all our trespasses, by canceling the record of debt that stood against us with its legal demands. This he set aside, nailing it to thecross. He disarmed the rulers and authorities and put them to open shame, by triumphing over them in him."

Forgiven – *charizomai* – means *"to bestow a favor unconditionally,"* is used in the act of *"forgiveness."*

Canceling – *exaleipho* – means *"to wipe away, wipe off, obliterate."*

Disarmed – *apekdyomai* – means *"to strip of arms, weapons."*

Triumphing – *thriambeuo* – means *"to celebrate a triumph over someone, to celebrate a victory."*

When Jesus hung on the Cross, He gave us two things: First, provision for all our needs for our:

- *Body* (healing, miracles, financial, materials, clothes, etc.)
- *Soul* (emotions, feelings, inner healing, and deliverance, etc.)
- *Spirit* (revelation, spiritual freedom, salvation, redemption, gifts, etc.)

In other words, complete salvation and redemption. Secondly, He gave us a complete, finished, irreversible, irrevocable victory over Satan and his works.

Again, have you abdicated your authority? Have you relinquished the throne God has given you? Have you given up on the power given to you through the Holy Spirit? How about the responsibility to give as you have received?

The way we retake our authority is as simple as saying a prayer, believing in our hearts the work of Jesus Christ that is irrevocable and irreversible. You and I continually wage war against unbelief and doubt in our lives until we see the manifestation of the provision Jesus made on the Cross for our lives. Declare and decree that you abdicate the kingdom of darkness and will no longer live under the rule of Satan and his works.

THE WORKS

The primary work of Jesus Christ was that of the Lamb of God. John 1:29 says, *"Behold, the Lamb of God, who takes away the sin of the world!"* Jesus came to earth to be the perfect lamb that we would have access to His perfect and redemptive work on the Cross to be reconciled to God the Father. Part of that reconciling work was for us to have the right to become children of God.

John 1:12-13 says,

> "But to all who did receive him, who believed in his name, he gave the right to become children of God, who were born, not of blood nor of the will of the flesh nor of the will of man, but of God." The reason we have authority given to us is that we have been given the right to be children.

This is a powerful revelation we must understand. This scripture clearly says that we were *"born, not of blood nor of the will of man, but of God."* Our mother birthed you and me, but according to scripture, we are born of God, when we repent of our sins and transgressions against God.

In the Church today, we have an identity and son-ship crisis. What do I mean by this? We have orphans working with a slave mentality, rather than Sons and Daughters doing the works of the Father. If we are to do the works of Jesus, we must do them as Children of God, for in it, is freedom and true identity.

John 14:12 says,

> "Truly, truly, I say to you, whoever believes in me will also do the works that I do; and greater works than these will he do, because I am going to the Father."

INTRODUCTION | A LONG BUT IMPORTANT ONE

Jesus did other works, although the primary one (salvation of humanity) could only be done by Him and through Him. He demonstrated other aspects of His ministry that we have been entrusted with, like:

- Teaching
- Preaching
- Healing
- Miracles
- Deliverance
- Intercession

These works or aspects of ministry are to be done by every son and daughter of God. He said we would do this and even greater things.

THE ANOINTING

In Luke 4:18-19, we see Jesus declaring the fulfillment of a prophecy given by the Prophet Isaiah (Read Isaiah 61). It says:

"The Spirit of the Lord is upon me, because he has anointed me to proclaim good news to the poor.

He has sent me to proclaim liberty to the captives and recovering of sight to the blind, to set at liberty those who are oppressed, 19 to proclaim the year of the Lord's favor."

The anointing has six major powers and purposes:

1. Preach and Proclaim the Good News of The Gospel to the poor.
2. Heal the brokenhearted
3. Deliverance to captives
4. Sight to the blind

5. Liberty to those who are captive

6. God's favor and ministry of reconciliation.

It's important that we understand the purpose of the anointing and that we don't lose sight of why God has anointed us. Jesus never exercised His call for self-promotion or benefit. Jesus came as a servant, to give His life for others. We, in the same way, use the anointing of God to serve, to lay down our lives as a living sacrifice unto God, that He may be glorified through every miracle, healing, and deliverance.

The anointing is also a great and powerful gift of God. It will many times give you access, but unless you have the character of Christ in your life, you will see great doors shut and your life destroyed by those character issues. It's important that we develop a Christ-like character of patience, holiness, long-suffering, endurance, and perseverance.

Don't put the anointing above character. Use Godly character as the foundation and roof of your house, as materials to build a strong wall to contain and release the anointing of God.

THE NAME

Jesus declared that we as sons and daughters have the authority to in His name *"cast out demons..."* *"heal the sick,"* etc...

Mark 16:17 "And these signs will accompany those who believe: in my name, they will cast out demons; they will speak in new tongues;"

Acts 16:17 "And this she kept doing for many days. Paul, having become greatly annoyed, turned and said to the spirit, 'I command you in the name of Jesus Christ to come out of her.' And it came out that very hour.

Acts 4:5-10 "On the next day their rulers and elders and scribes gathered together in Jerusalem, 6 with Annas the high priest and Caiaphas and John and Alexander, and all who were of the high-priestly family. 7 And when they had set them in the midst, they inquired, 'By what power or by what name did you do this?' 8 Then Peter, filled with the Holy Spirit, said to them, "Rulers of the people and elders, 9 if we are being examined today concerning a good deed done to a crippled man, by what means this man has been healed, 10 let it be known to all of you and to all the people of Israel that by the name of Jesus Christ of Nazareth, whom you crucified, whom God raised from the dead—by him this man is standing before you well."

When a son or daughter of God uses the name of Jesus, Heaven and Earth listen. Sickness, demons, and circumstances must shift. We have authority to use the name of Jesus Christ of Nazareth.

THE HOLY SPIRIT

Matthew 12:28 "But if it is by the Spirit of God that I cast out demons, then the kingdom of God has come upon you."

Luke 11:20 "But if it is by the finger of God that I cast out demons, then the kingdom of God has come upon you."

The ministry of casting out demons (Deliverance) is one of the most controversial ministries today as it was in the days of Jesus. The religious man of the day had never seen such an increase in the manifestations of deliverance like they did when Jesus ministered.

The closest thing they had to this manifestation attributed to God in the Old Testament was David playing his instrument in the presence of Saul and an oppressing spirit leaving whenever he did that (Read 1 Samuel 16:14-23).

The measure of deliverance they had experienced, was of relief and not complete freedom like Jesus was demonstrating.

They marveled at Jesus authority over demonic spirits. They thought it had to be by the hand of the enemy himself, the prince of demons. Therefore, they attributed the work of deliverance to Beelzebub (Read 2 Kings 1:2).

> Luke 11:14-15 "Now he was casting out a demon that was mute. When the demon had gone out, the mute man spoke, and the people marveled. 15 But some of them said, 'He casts out demons by Beelzebul, the prince of demons'."

Jesus declares that it was by the Holy Spirit that He had authority to cast out demons. The Gospel of Luke says, "by the finger of God" (Read Exodus 8:19), this is about the work of the Holy Spirit. We, by the Holy Spirit, have authority to command demons to come out and leave.

THE WORD

> Matthew 8:16 "That evening they brought to him many who were oppressed by demons, and he cast out the spirits with a word and healed all who were sick."

> Luke 4:32 "And he went down to Capernaum, a city of Galilee. And he was teaching them on the Sabbath, 32 and they were as-

tonished at his teaching, for his word possessed authority. 33 And in the synagogue, there was a man who had the spirit of an unclean demon, and he cried out with a loud voice, 34 'Ha! What have you to do with us, Jesus of Nazareth? Have you come to destroy us? I know who you are—the Holy One of God.' 35 But Jesus rebuked him, saying, 'Be silent and come out of him!' And when the demon had thrown him down in their midst, he came out of him, having done him no harm."

When Jesus dealt with demonic powers, He did not go into a sermon message or counseling session. He commanded them with a word, and they came out. We have authority to command demons to come out with the Word of God, and they must obey.

THE KEY

John 15:13 "Greater love has no one than this, that someone lay down his life for his friends."

Real Spiritual Authority comes from surrender and submission to the Authority of Christ. The more we surrender to the Authority of Christ in our lives, the more we are empowered to live for Him and through Him.

When you look at your life, look at the areas that are not under the Authority of Christ, and you will see the works of Satan manifesting. Stealing, killing, and destroying, when you have the Authority of Christ in those areas, you will see life and life more abundant (John 10:10).

The Apostle Paul said it this way

"I have been crucified with Christ. It is no longer I who live, but Christ who lives in me. And the life I now live in the flesh I live by

faith in the Son of God, who loved me and gave himself for me."
(Galatians 2:20)

I surrendered unto Him all there was of me; everything! Then for the first time, I realized what it meant to have real power. - Kathryn Kuhlman

The key is to surrender. Retake your authority through Christ and exercise it.

Prayer: Father God, I repent for abdicating your Kingdom and Authority given to me. I renounce and repent for relinquishing my rightful place. I surrender to you every area that I have taken control of, or areas I've surrendered to the enemy. Holy Spirit I ask that you empower me, that you deliver me, and that you lead me to victory. Jesus, I thank you for your blood, for your provision, and irrevocable, irreversible victory on the Cross for me. Amen.

CHAPTER 1

THE MINISTRY OF JESUS

"In Jesus' mind, a normal assignment for His followers was to go out and spread the message of the kingdom of God by, among other things, casting out demons. He sent out the 12 apostles with 'power over unclean spirits, to cast them out' (Matt. 10:1). He later sent out 70 disciples, and they 'returned with joy, saying, 'Lord, even the demons are subject to us in Your name' (Luke 10:17). Jesus then said, 'These signs will follow those who believe: In My name, they will cast out demons' (Mark 16:17)."

-C. Peter Wagner

7 Power Principles I Learned after Seminary

Along the way, as you exercise the authority given by God to deliver the captive and heal the sick. You will face demonic spirits that oppress and possess people. The revelation of the ministry of deliverance is vital and necessary for the Body of Christ today. It is one of the most controversial ministries. It is also one of the least exercised in the Church today.

THE MINISTRY OF JESUS

Matthew 4:23-24 (AMP) says,

"23 And He went about all Galilee, teaching in their synagogues and preaching the good news (Gospel) of the kingdom, and healing every disease and every weakness and infirmity among the people. 24 So the report of Him spread throughout all Syria, and they brought Him all who were sick, those afflicted with various diseases and torments, those under the power of demons, and epileptics, and paralyzed people, and He healed them."

Mark 1:39 (ESV) says,

"And he went throughout all Galilee, preaching in their synagogues and casting out demons."

4 Things Jesus Did Wherever He Went:
1. He Preached
2. He Taught
3. He Healed
4. He Cast out Demons.

The first three are very common in the Church. We have pastors preaching, teaching, and praying for the sick. The reason we do not see the ministry of deliverance exercised is, as I mentioned in the previous lesson, we have abdicated our authority as believers.

We must take it back and exercise our authority in Jesus to cast out demons. The full ministry of Jesus was not just preaching, teaching, and healing; it included setting the captives free from demonic forces. He exercised this often and its one of the reasons the religious systems of the day resisted the ministry of Jesus.

Today, because many lack the understanding and purpose of deliverance, they resist and live under oppression themselves. Jesus delivered the captives in His day, and He still does today. We need a correct understanding of this ministry today, so many can experience the full benefits of the Kingdom of God.

WHAT IS DELIVERANCE?

In order for us to be effective believers in our ministry, we must understand the power and authority given to us to bring freedom. The Apostle Paul said, *"For we do not wrestle against flesh and blood, but against the rulers, against the authorities, against the cosmic powers over this present darkness, against the spiritual forces of evil in the heavenly places."* Ephesians 6:12-13 Our warfare is not against flesh and blood. Often, we are faced with problems in relationships, business, ministry and just life in general, the cause behind these issues may not be natural, but a spiritual force behind it.

I define Deliverance as *"The permanent removal of demonic powers and the elimination of every system, door or oppressions that feed them by closing all access points to the enemy."*

Deliverance is not limited to the ministry of individual people; it includes families, cities or nations. No matter what deliverance affects, the most vital and important aspect of it is the removal of lifelines that allow cycles or continuity of its works.

For example, a person who has been sexually abused must go through the process of forgiving their abuser so that demonic spirits that have gained access can be evicted. At the same time, close all points of access for it to never return. Processes like this, can sometimes take time.

Another important aspect of deliverance is understanding that we are called to engage in spiritual warfare. Jesus said, *"But if it is by the finger of God that I cast out demons, then the kingdom of God has come upon you."* (Luke 11:20, ESV) Deliverance brings about a spiritual conflict between God's Dominion and the Satan's works. This is what we call spiritual warfare. Deliverance is what initiated this conflict, and sometimes it manifests in the natural.

WHAT IS SPIRITUAL WARFARE?

Unfortunately, spiritual warfare is not a very popular topic in the Church today. It's unfortunate because scripture presents evidence that spiritual warfare is a reality we face as believers. An over-emphasis of spiritual warfare can lead to attributing every sin, habit, or problem to demonic influence.

Under-emphasizing it can be as dangerous, as the enemy would love nothing more than to keep every saint ignorant of his schemes (2 Cor. 2:10-11; Ephesians 6:11). Whatever belief you currently hold to, you cannot ignore it. Dr. Bill Hamon says that many Christians have an unspoken covenant with the enemy, which says if you don't bother me, I won't bother you! It's time to break up this unspoken covenant!

SPIRITUAL WARFARE AND THE LIFE OF THE BELIEVER

Many of the terms used to describe the life of the believer are militant terms that we cannot ignore.

> "This charge I entrust to you, Timothy, my child, in accordance with the prophecies previously made about you, that by them you may wage the good warfare, holding faith and a good conscience. By rejecting this, some have made shipwreck of their faith," (1 Timothy 1:18–19, ESV)

The Apostle Paul gives a clear warning to Timothy; those who neglect to hold on to faith and a good conscience end up shipwrecked, but it is the result of not engaging in the realm of warfare where we can obtain victories that keep our faith footed and our conscience pure.

> "Therefore, humble yourselves under the mighty hand of God, so that at the right time he may lift you up. Throw all your anxieties upon him, because he cares about you. Stay sober, stay alert! Your enemy, the Adversary, stalks about like a roaring lion looking for someone to devour. Stand against him, firm in your trust, knowing that your brothers throughout the world are going through the same kinds of suffering." (1 Peter 5:6–9, CJB)

Spiritual warfare takes place in two phases that go hand-in-hand. It's the process of transformation that every person goes through; it happens simultaneously and always begins with recognizing the need to be transformed. Apostle Peter said, "Therefore, humble yourselves under the mighty hand of God."

It is the recognition that we must be under His (God) Kingdom and in His will that initiates the greatest spiritual conflict that can take place between the Kingdom of God and the kingdom of Satan. As we enter into the place of surrender, we begin to see the removal of demonic influence, the forsaking of sin, the radical transformation of our minds and lifestyle. The Apostle Peter, warns us to always be alert and to stand against him. Spiritual warfare does not end when we are saved; it is the beginning of a lifestyle that utterly opposes every work of Satan.

As Children of God, we are called to engage in spiritual warfare to the extent that others can experience the same freedom we are experiencing in life. It means engaging through the authority and power of the Holy Spirit in the removal of everything that stands in the way of God and Souls, nations, families, and cities.

SPIRITUAL NOT NATURAL

"For we do not wrestle against flesh and blood, but against the rulers, against the authorities, against the cosmic powers over this present darkness, against the spiritual forces of evil in the heavenly places." (Ephesians 6:12, ESV)

We must remember that it is *"SPIRITUAL"* not *"NATURAL"* warfare we are engaging in. When we don't understand that it's spiritual we participate in natural warfare through gossip, murmuring, criticism, offenses, etc. Such things have a spiritual root, and we will not win over them unless we address them in heart and spirit. Leonard Ravenhill said, "God doesn't listen to gossip except to judge it." He also said, "Notice, we never pray for folks we gossip about, and we never gossip about the folk for whom we pray! For prayer is a great deterrent."

IT'S TIME TO ENLIST IN GOD'S SPIRITUAL ARMY

"You then, my child, be strengthened by the grace that is in Christ Jesus, and what you have heard from me in the presence of many witnesses entrust to faithful men, who will be able to teach others also. Share in suffering as a good soldier of Christ Jesus. No soldier gets entangled in civilian pursuits, since his aim is to please the one who enlisted him." (2 Timothy 2:1–4, ESV)

Are you still a civilian in the Kingdom of God? If you are, it's time to enlist in God's Army. An army that has already won at the Cross through the mighty work of Christ, our Commander-in-Chief. You are not part of a defeated army; you are part of a victorious army! The victory Christ obtained for us is

- IRREVERSIBLE
- IRREVOCABLE
- FINAL!

PROCLAIMING THE GOSPEL

Matthew 3:1-2 says that John the Baptist preached, "Repent, for the kingdom of heaven is at hand." Jesus said in regard to John the Baptist and the Kingdom in Matthew 11:12 "From the days of John the Baptist until now the kingdom of heaven has suffered violence, and the violent take it by force." When Jesus made this declaration, it was because John the Baptist was the first one to preach the Kingdom. It was at this moment the confrontation started to take place between the Kingdom of God and the kingdom of darkness.

When we preach the Kingdom of God, the conflict manifests through deliverance, and yet this is one of the least seen today because the Gospel has been partially proclaimed. It can only mean the Gospel has been watered down, it's been diluted to the point it has no effect in impacting the hearts of man, and even demons don't tremble at it anymore.

Jesus himself started His ministry by preaching the same message that John the Baptist proclaimed. He said in Mark 1:15, *"and saying, "The time is fulfilled, and the kingdom of God is at hand; repent and believe in the gospel."* If Jesus went about teaching and preaching about His Kingdom and the fruit was healing, deliverance, Heaven on Earth, then how much more should we preach it and proclaim it.

Later on, in Verses 21-28 in Chapter 1 of Mark, we see that conflict manifest as Jesus is teaching in a synagogue. But He was not just teaching and preaching. He was doing it with authority.

It says in the Amplified Version, *"And they were completely astonished at His teaching, for He was teaching as One Who possessed authority and not as the scribes."*

Frank Hammond says about this passage, *"A watered down, social gospel may not offend men but neither does it offend demons! However, strong, authoritative teaching spoken in faith causes every demon present to tremble."*

THE TRILLION DOLLAR QUESTION

At the core of deliverance ministry, we find the issue of possession versus oppression. This is a critical issue that deserves an accurate answer to bring a balanced and proper foundation to the ministry of deliverance.

Deliverance ministry has had its controversies. Debates have ranged from the method to delivering the captives to the trillion-dollar question if demons can possess a born-again believer.

These arguments have come about because of lack of knowledge and improper teaching, and it's one of the main reasons abuses take place in this ministry.

The answer to this question will vary depending on a person's experience, theological beliefs, and personal study of scripture. To address this issue appropriately, it would take a book on its own.

When we use the term *"possession,"* it communicates the idea of ownership and complete control of a person. To many, immediately scenes from the Exorcist come to mind. Unfortunately, this very idea has caused many to reject the ministry of deliverance. Can demonic manifestations like such happen? Of course, scripture gives us vivid accounts of such events, but does one scriptural account define all?

New Testament Scholar Clinton E. Arnold explains one of the leading causes of confusion:

"I wholeheartedly agree with this conclusion. A Christian cannot be owned and controlled by a demon. What many people do not realize, however, is that the word possession never even appears in the Bible in the passages where Jesus or the apostles cast evil spirits out of an individual. The expression demon- possessed or demon possession does occur in some English translations of the Greek text, but there is never a Greek word for 'possession' that stands behind it. 'Demon possession' is always the translation of a single Greek word, daimonizomai. Words for ownership or possession (e.g., huparchō, echō, katechō, ktaomai, or peripoieō) are absent in the original text. The idea of possession is the interpretation of the Greek term by Bible translators. This translation of the word became standard because the most popular English Bible translation for over three centuries—the King James Version—used 'demon possession' or 'possessed with the devil' to render the Greek.

Clinton E. Arnold, further explains where we got the idea of possession:

Where did English Bible translators get the idea of translating daimonizomai as "demon possession"? The translation was most likely influenced by the Latin church's tradition of using the term possessio to describe a person deeply troubled by a demonic spirit.

Interestingly, the Latin Vulgate, however, does not use the term possessio to translate daimonizomai, but the simple expression to have a demon (habeo with daemonia). But it is also important to realize that the English term possess has a long history of usage where the emphasis could fall on control or occupancy as opposed to ownership. This is significant because it is by no means certain that the translators of the King James Version intended to convey the notion of ownership by using the term possession.

The obstacle for us is that in popular contemporary usage we have a difficult time disentangling possession from the concept of ownership. As we can see, the idea and question that a born-again believer can be possessed are founded at best on a misunderstanding of how the original Greek was translated and at worse wrongly translated.

Scripture clearly says that the Blood of Christ has purchased us and that we are the Temple of the Holy Spirit. (1 Peter 1:18-19 & 1 Corinthians 6:19-20)

Dr. Arnold suggests a different way of asking to arrive at a more sound and biblical conclusion in defining the operation of demons in the life of a born-again Christian:

"We might ask," he says, 'Can Christians come under a high degree of influence by a demonic spirit?' or, 'Is it possible for Christians to yield control of their bodies to a demonic spirit in the same way that they yield to the power of sin?'"

In answer to his question, I believe it is possible. Many areas of the life of a believer can be under the influence of demons that result in sickness, addictions, poverty, depression, suicides, sexual addiction, and many other works of oppression by demonic spirits.

This means these areas are not submitted to the Lordship of Jesus, and that is the reason why they are under the influence/oppression of demons. Dr. Arnold describes how demons can affect a believer.

When a person becomes a Christian, Christ dwells in his or her heart, but sin is still present. "The point is that Christ wants to assert his lordship over every room of the house. He wants to dwell in all the rooms and be the most important influence in each. Believers need to open the door of each room to him and allow him to clean out the defilements, chase out any illegal occupants, and rebuild and redecorate the rooms."

Christ dwells in our living room, our spirit-heart. But what about the rest of the rooms, like our bed-room (sexuality), kitchen (relationships), entertain-ment room (social life), etc. Any area that is unsurren-dered can be influenced by spirits that can oppress and bring destruction.

One of the fears especially if we think posses-sion instead of degrees of influence is the fact that we may lose our salvation. Again Clinton E. Arnold explains in his book, 3 Crucial Questions about Spiri-tual Warfare:

"In ancient Israel, the temple of the Lord remained the Lord's house in spite of various kings bringing in defiling and impure objects.

Our bodies and our very beings belong to the Lord regardless of the compromises we make and the defilements we yield to and allow into our lives. Like the godly kings of Israel, we need to clean the garbage out of the temple and break the unholy allegiances. The apostle John assures us that Jesus keeps the believer safe "and the evil one cannot harm him" (1 John 5:18). No one, including Satan or any of his host, can separate us from the love of God and steal from us our precious salvation. But we can allow demons a signifi-cant amount of turf, which they are all too happy to take, and they can exercise a high degree of influence and control."

In conclusion, possession would mean that our redeemed spirit could be controlled by demons even when the Holy Spirit resides there, but this is un-scriptural. The more scriptural understanding is that a born-again believer through their willful disobedi-ence and unsurrendered areas of their life can give access to the operation of demonic influence to such an extent that they can be oppressed and be given control in certain areas of their life.

There is much to learn about the ministry of deliverance. We must continually seek God for revelation and understanding. But we must not be afraid to exercise this great weapon of war that God has entrusted us with. The believer has authority and must not shy away from the spiritual warfare they are facing. Revelation knowledge is vital and essential to be an effective believer, but that revelation knowledge not put into action is dead.

PRACTICAL WAYS TO ACTIVATETHE MINISTRY OF DELIVERANCE

UNDERSTAND YOUR SPIRITUAL AUTHORITY

Understanding and Revelation precede manifestation. Frequently saints want to see the demonstration of the Kingdom of God in their life without having a proper foundation and revelation of the Kingdom. At the same time, we cannot wait until we have all the knowledge and revelation to engage in the ministry of deliverance.

EXERCISE YOUR SPIRITUAL AUTHORITY

One practical way you can begin to exercise your spiritual authority is to take every opportunity to offer the gift of freedom to people. When you see oppression believe God for favor to bring freedom and declare freedom over them.

CHAPTER 2

FORGIVENESS & ACCEPTANCE

"There is a sin that cannot be forgiven unless a person takes certain actions. In the Lord's Prayer that Jesus taught His disciples, He included this statement; "Forgive us our trespasses as we forgive those who trespass against us." Jesus is saying that God will only forgive us to the degree that we forgive others, for at the end of the Lord's Prayer in Mt. 6:9–13 He makes this declaration in verse 14 & 15. "For if you forgive men their trespasses, your heavenly Father will also forgive you. But if you do not forgive men their trespasses, neither will your Father forgive your trespasses." This is stated by Jesus Himself that God the Father cannot and will not forgive the sin of unforgiveness."

-Bill Hamon

How Can These Things Be?: A Preacher and a Miracle Worker but Denied Heaven!

"To carry a grudge is like being stung to death by one bee." - William H. Walton

Every day we face challenges, we face an ever-increasing opportunity for offense and un- forgiveness that can imprison our heart. Forgiveness, is one of the least talked about topics in friendships, families, workplaces, and Churches.

When we mention it, most become defensive about it. No one wants to be known as having unforgiveness towards someone else. We all face it every day..

What can cause Unforgiveness and Offense?

- Betrayals
- Rejection
- Prejudices
- Divorce
- Abandonment
- Gossip
- Grudges
- Resentment
- Sexual Abuse
- Someone ignores you
- Much more.

Opportunity for offense and unforgiveness are always around us.

Matthew 18:7 says,

"Woe to the world because of offenses! For offenses must come, but woe to that man by whom the offense comes!" There is no way to avoid offenses; they always present themselves. But we do have a choice whether we allow those offenses to become roots of unforgiveness and bitterness.

The word offense here is skandalon meaning a trap, snare, bait to cause you to stumble. When someone hurts you, offends you, there is a decision to be made. You can take the bait of the enemy that says you have a right to be offended or forgive and restore the relationship.

Let me give you an example. Growing up, I had a lot of anger and hatred in my heart. I used to get easily upset and misunderstand everything said to me. Obviously, I had already gone beyond the point of an offense, and I had bitterness and unforgiveness in my heart. But I remember, the day I chose not to take the bait. I was driving; a family member was with me. This family member said something that could have triggered the anger and hatred again. Now I don't know if they meant to do it on purpose, but I remember I had chosen before getting in that car, "I will not take any bait" or give occasion for things to get triggered.

I noticed two things happened, one, I did not get angry and explode as I used to do. Secondly, they could not continue because I had taken power away from the offense. I had forgiven and chosen at that moment that I would not allow things to be triggered. We have more self-control than we realize and at the same time the power of this fruit of the spirit can render powerless any form of bondage in your life!

Your response to the offense can either escalate things or diffuse it. There is power and freedom in a forgiven heart. This may seem like something small in your eyes, but nonetheless, some relationships end because of lack of forgiveness towards offenses.

When we have a forgiven heart, we don't easily take the bait; we see the traps set out by the enemy that cause destruction in our families and relationships.

FORGIVE OTHERS

Your father and mother abandoned you, your uncle and aunt abused you, your boss embarrassed you. We can get hurt in life, but to not forgive others will only keep you captive in torment and darkness. I have experienced it. When I was a kid, I was abused a lot, verbally and physically. I hated others for it, and I was filled with rage and anger because of what they had done. Mainly I could not believe my parents had not been there for me. But I found out quickly I was only keeping myself in a prison of resentment and bitterness.

When I realized the power of forgiveness, I was free. The rage and anger that had control over me could no longer overpower me. I remember that my bitterness and resentment was hurting me more than my family. Yes, they were hurt by my actions of hate and rage against them, but I was only digging myself a grave of death.

When you meet forgiveness, you meet her power, the power of freedom. Her fruit is sweet and sets you free. Over the next few pages, as you read every word. I will share with you testimonies and keys to experiencing such a forgiven heart. Join me....

Testimony: Forgiveness, Her Fruit is Deliverance!

I was on a weekend camp with young people last year. I was the guest speaker for the week. Almost everyone was receiving from God in an amazing way, except for one particular young man; I could tell he was struggling to receive. That weekend I focused on freedom from rejection and unforgiveness. Every day, with every message, I could see the fruit of God's power healing, restoring, and delivering them. But this young man was not receiving at all. I knew there was something wrong. I said, "Lord, only you can do something, even at the last-minute." As we packed, getting ready to go back into the city, from a beautiful mountain retreat, this young man and his brother got to ride on the same car I was going in. I said, "This is it!" As we were driving back, I prayed to myself, "Lord show me something that will open his heart." I had a bag of M&M's in my bag, so I took it out, opened it and offered him and his brother some. I said to him "Tell me about your father." The young man began to weep uncontrollably. He had unforgiveness towards his father because of abandonment and the divorce his parents went through. He felt his father had rejected him. After I had led him on a prayer of forgiveness towards his dad, his eyes lit up, he had a huge smile on his face. His countenance of anger and rage changed to one of freedom.

FORGIVE YOURSELF!

I had to forgive myself. Sometimes we can blame ourselves for so many things. You can blame yourself because you did not do well enough in your last job review to get a raise. You blame yourself because you were not careful and that is why you had a car accident, and now you are living in pain. You blame yourself because you allowed certain things to happen when you could have done something about it.

All the self-blame, accusation and rejection are tormentors, accusing and keeping you bound in darkness. When you forgive yourself, you discover His grace and mercy in your life. As I mentioned before,

I had dug a grave for myself. I had gone into such a deep depression and rage that I had become suicidal. My heart now breaks for young people, trapped in prisons of un-forgiveness towards themselves. I want to tell you there is real freedom!

Testimony: Forgiveness, Her Fruit is Healing!

On a Friday night ministry time at my family church, I was praying for a lady's knee to be healed. My friend and I prayed, she felt something, but not complete healing. I asked her how she hurt her knee. She went on to say "I was not careful, I have always believed God for healing, this time I gave into the doctor's suggestion for surgery. I stopped believing God; I should have believed Him for my healing." I could sense the blame she was putting on herself. I said to her "It's OK. You can believe Him now for it; just pray this prayer with me." I led her in a prayer of self-forgiveness.

My friend and I prayed for her again, and immediately her healing came. We had her stand, walk, then run. Before you knew it, everyone was watching her walking fast and running around the sanctuary of the Church. Unforgiveness towards self can hold our miracles captive. Forgive yourself!

I can share with you many testimonies like this. Forgiving yourself can bring not only miracles, but also freedom from the past. Just a few nights ago my team in Prophetic Healing and Deliverance ministered to two different people in the area of forgiveness. One person was filled with shame and unforgiveness towards self. The other person was bound with blame because he could not believe how many years he has struggled with mental issues, addictions, and bondage. Both individuals received their freedom.

FORGIVE GOD!

How about God? Did He abandon us? Did he forget about us? No! The devil is a deceiver, and he only knows how to lie. You cannot believe any of his lies. He will make you question God all day long about why he let someone hurt you or why you went through abuse when you were a child. It's all lies, and plans to keep you in prisons of torment.

Does God need forgiveness? I believe He does not, but we need to forgive for our inner healing and freedom.

Testimony: Forgiveness, Her Fruit is Intimacy with Father God!

One of my biggest struggles growing up was to believe that God truly loved me as a Father. I was abused over and over by father figures. My earthly father never abused me but was absent. So those that had taken his role distorted that view. I was angry at God, and I remember going through a time of deliverance, where I saw myself in a vision hiding behind a wall when I was a little kid. I poked my head out while keeping my body behind the wall still. I saw what to me was the Father extending His hands towards me.

I was confused by my emotions. I felt angry, yet in desperate need to be embraced by Him. After this vision, I realized my unforgiveness towards God was that wall. I would poke my head out occasionally just to be sure that God was still there. But I would keep myself behind it still. I remember I began to weep uncontrollably because I knew I had to forgive those that distorted my view of Father God. He never hurt me. He never abandoned me. But I had held an offense against Him because of others. I had to forgive others and God so that I could receive His forgiveness towards me. After weeping for what seemed to me forever, I felt closer to Him. Ever since that moment, I have felt so much closer to Him. Before I refused to allow joy, peace, and love to be expressed from God towards me. Now it's my number one desire. I find rest in Him. I know I'm His son, He is my Father, and He loves me!

I believe this is your time for forgiveness. There is a need for a revival of repentance and forgiveness in the Body of Christ. We for too long have stuffed bitterness, resentment, and unforgiveness towards others. Instead of coming before God and confessing our hardness of heart and tasting of the sweetness of His forgiving fruit!

WHAT IS FORGIVENESS?

"A forgiveness ought to be like a canceled note, torn in two and burned up, so that it can never be shown against the man." -Henry Ward Beecher

Forgiveness means to grant someone a pardon for an offense they have caused against you. To pardon them, to let go of the offense, without the need of them making amends for whatever they did to you. Forgiveness is a decision, choosing to forgive, pardon, and erase the debt they owe you.

In the Greek, the word means to *graciously restore one to another, to bestow, to favor them, to kindly give freely something they do not deserve, but you choose to do it anyways.*

Adam and Eve lived a life of freedom when they walked with God. They did not even need to know what forgiveness was. When they disobeyed God's original mandate, they offended God; they incurred a debt, they had never experienced debt, wrongdoing, sin, or missing the mark until they disobeyed Him.

God could at that very moment have chosen to call in their debt, but rather, He chose to forgive. Father, Son, and Holy Spirit gathered to carry out the eternal plan of forgiveness. Jesus looking at the Father said, *'I will go, walk among them, become a perfect living sacrifice for their forgiveness, I will take upon myself and become sin for their forgiveness.'* (Acts 13:38; Ephesians 1:7).

The Father probably said, *"Not yet; there is an appointed time. When that time comes, I will reveal to them my love through you, and they will have eternal life through you. I will forgive their sins, offenses, and unforgiveness if they repent and believe in you, that I sent you; so that they will love one another again and live in relationship with me."* (1 John 4:9-11)

Meanwhile, the Holy Spirit, empowering the Patriarchs, Judges, Prophets (Acts 10:43) and Kings repeatedly released and proclaimed the coming of Jesus Christ, demonstrating a day of forgiveness in their fallen nature by the power of the Holy Spirit. Knowing that one day Jesus would hang on a cross and He, the Holy Spirit, would resurrect Him from the grave, and later become our advocate and helper in understanding the Power of Jesus to forgive us our sins (Acts 2:38).

God had the opportunity not to forgive, but He instead began a plan for restoration and forgiveness. Forgiveness is not something to take lightly; it's important in our daily walk towards freedom. Jesus hung on a cross and died, resurrected from the dead to forgive our sins, cancel our debt towards God, heal our bodies from death and infirmity, to set us free from torment.

Do you have poverty in your life? Sickness? Bondage of Sin? Unforgiveness can hold your freedom captive until you choose to forgive and be forgiven.

THE GOOD NEWS

One of my favorite Gospels is Mark. It starts right away with the core message of the Kingdom of God; Repentance and Forgiveness.

Mark 1:4

4 John came baptizing in the wilderness and preaching a baptism of repentance for the forgiveness of sins. 14 After John was arrested, Jesus went to Galilee, preaching the good news of God: 15 "The time is fulfilled, and the kingdom of God has come near. Repent and believe in the good news!"

Mark 2:5-17

5 Seeing their faith, Jesus told the paralytic, "Son, your sins are forgiven." 6 But some of the scribes were sitting there, thinking to themselves: 7 "Why does He speak like this? He's blaspheming! Who can forgive sins but God alone?" 8 Right away Jesus understood in His spirit that they were reasoning like this within themselves and said to them, "Why are you reasoning these things in your hearts? 9 Which is easier: to say to the paralytic, 'Your sins are forgiven,' or to say, 'Get up, pick up your stretcher, and walk '? 10 But so you may know that the Son of Man has authority on earth to forgive sins," He told the paralytic, 11 "I tell you: get up, pick up your stretcher, and go home."12 Immediately he got up, picked up the stretcher, and went out in front of everyone. As a result, they were all astounded and gave glory to God, saying, "We have never seen anything like this!" 15 While He was reclining at the table in Levi's house, many tax collectors and sinners were also guests with Jesus and His disciples, because there were many who were following Him. 16 When the scribes of the Pharisees saw that He was eating with sinners and tax collectors, they asked His disciples, "Why does He eat with tax collectors and sinners?"17 When Jesus heard this, He told them, "Those who are well don't need a doctor, but the sick [do need one]. I didn't come to call the righteous, but sinners."

WHAT IS THE GOOD NEWS OF THE KINGDOM?

The good news is, when you repent, you can be forgiven. Jesus shed His blood, for the forgiveness of your sins, if you don't forgive others, He cannot forgive you. You can't believe the Good News; give the Good News, unless you have been forgiven.

THE GIFT OF FORGIVENESS

"To err is human, to forgive, divine." Alexander Pope

John 4 tells us about the encounter with Jesus and the Samaritan woman at the well. Jesus asks her for water, and she immediately points out the obvious; you are a Jew, and you don't associate with us Samaritans. "Why are you asking me for water?" she asks. Jesus says to her, "If you knew the gift of God, and who is saying to you, 'Give Me a drink,' you would ask Him, and He would give you living water." The Gift of God, forgiveness from anything, no matter what your social status may be, forgiveness from your past, sin, from anything that may seem impossible to you to forgive.

She still did not understand what Jesus was referring to, her natural mind, her natural sense of indifference and resentment between the Jewish and Samaritans was preventing her from receiving the Gift of God. She once again points out the obvious, "Sir," said the woman, "You don't even have a bucket, and the well is deep. So where do you get this 'living water'?"

Jesus said,

"Everyone who drinks from this water will get thirsty again. 14 But whoever drinks from the water that I will give him will never get thirsty again—ever! In fact, the water I will give him will become a well of water springing up within him for eternal life." "Sir," the

> woman said to Him, "give me this water so I won't get thirsty and come here to draw water."

She continues to struggle to receive the revelation that Jesus is the Sacrifice for her sins and the giver of Forgiveness. Jesus forgives the woman's sin. The joy of her forgiven heart becomes contagious, turning a whole town upside down. Everyone knew who she was, the details of her past life, and they saw her forgiven heart. Thirsty for this living water of forgiveness, they all went out to see Jesus. The Disciples learn an invaluable lesson on the Gift of God for all humanity. They questioned the woman, "why are you talking to Him?" Our natural minds cannot comprehend forgiveness, and it must be a revelation and experience in our hearts. Let's read the rest of the account of this powerful encounter:

John 4 :16-42

> "Go call your husband," He told her, "and come back here." 17 "I don't have a husband," she answered. "You have correctly said, 'I don't have a husband,' "Jesus said. For you've had five husbands, and the man you now have is not your husband. What you have said is true." "Sir," the woman replied, "I see that You are a prophet. Our fathers worshiped on this mountain, yet you [Jews] say that the place to worship is in Jerusalem." Jesus told her, "Believe Me, woman, an hour is coming when you will worship the Father neither on this mountain nor in Jerusalem. You Samaritans worship what you do not know. We worship what we do know, because salvation is from the Jews. But an hour is coming, and is now here, when the true worshipers will worship the Father in spirit and truth. Yes, the Father wants such people to worship Him. God is spirit, and those who worship Him must worship in spirit and truth." The woman said to Him, "I know that Messiah is coming" (who is called Christ). "When He comes, He will explain everything to us." "I am [He]," Jesus told her, "the One speaking to you. Just then His disciples arrived, and they were amazed that He was talking with a woman. Yet no one said, "What do You want?" or "Why are You

talking with her?" Then the woman left her water jar, went into town, and told the men, "Come, see a man who told me everything I ever did! Could this be the Messiah?" They left the town and made their way to Him... Now many Samaritans from that town believed in Him because of what the woman said when she testified, "He told me everything I ever did." Therefore, when the Samaritans came to Him, they asked Him to stay with them, and He stayed there two days. Many more believed because of what He said. And they told the woman, "We no longer believe because of what you said, for we have heard for ourselves and know that this really is the Savior of the world."

When you experience true forgiveness, your joy and forgiven heart will become contagious.

HOW TO FORGIVE

Forgiveness is a daily walk in our everyday life. When we decide to have a forgiving heart, we may encounter some of the most difficult obstacles of our lives. Offenses and misunderstandings refine our heart; it tests our character and strength of relationships. We should not despise it, but rather embrace the power of forgiveness and walk it out hand in hand with others.

There are relationships where people are in danger, because of abuse and the like and believe they should take action to be safe, but the solution is not holding on to the unforgiveness, but rather to forgive and move forward with your life.

I could give you a step by step guide to praying to forgive, but the reality is, do you want to forgive? This is a question only you can answer, when you want to, you truly step into a place of forgiveness. Let me say, that sometimes we complicate this process; a simple prayer can begin your journey to total forgiveness.

Prayer to forgive:

> Father God, I come before you, first forgiving those that have offended me, I cannot be forgiven unless I forgive them first. Lord I cancel (name of people) debt, offense, need for him/her to make amends. I let them go from any judgments I have set against them. I repent for my unforgiveness. I ask for forgiveness for the bitterness and resentment. I renounce every demon of unforgiveness, bitterness, and resentment. I command you in the name of Jesus to let go of my emotions, body, and soul now in Jesus name. I forgive myself, and I command every spirit of blame and judgement to let go of my emotions, soul and body now. Father God, I ask now that you cleanse me of all resentment and bitterness. I ask that you fill me with your Holy Spirit, every void left, fill me with your presence and love. I declare I'm free, and I declare I'm forgiven, I declare those who offended me are free in Jesus name. Amen.

CHAPTER 3

INNER HEALING

"Often a deliverance session will turn up some demonizing influence from which the counselee is gloriously freed by the power of Christ. All are now rejoicing and saying, 'Praise the Lord,' because the house has been swept clean. But too often the unresolved hurts, the emotional trauma and, in the case of sin, the compromised will, have not been adequately dealt with. Unless sensitive counseling brings inner healing and closure to memories and attitudes, many of them on a subconscious level, the swept house will be reinvaded by its former evil tenant, and perhaps by many more." (see Luke 11:24-26).

C. Peter Wagner

Supernatural Forces in Spiritual Warfare

Isaiah 61:1 "The Spirit of the Lord God is upon me, because the Lord has anointed me to bring good news to the poor; he has sent me to bind up the brokenhearted, to proclaim liberty to the captives, and the opening of the prison to those who are bound."

WHAT IS INNER HEALING?

Deliverance is the eviction and removal of demonic possession or influence over the life of a person. Inner healing is the subsequent step to complete the process of deliverance and healing of the individual.

Inner healing is the process of healing our inner man (soul/ spirit). Our soul man is the seat of emotions, memories, thoughts, and beliefs. More on that later. Deliverance is never complete without the process of inner healing. Often due to lack of knowledge of how God has designed us, we strive to deal with demonic influence first and believe that the moment it's been removed, we no longer need any further ministry. But first, let me share with you an illustration that will help us see the difference between deliverance (eviction of demonic influence) versus inner healing (healing of the inner man).

ILLUSTRATION | INFECTED WOUND | REMOVING SCAR TISSUE

Imagine for a second that a wound got infected in your arm, the wound was a result of an accident or harm done purposely by someone. The infection is a consequence of the injury or damage, and the infection of the wound must be removed. Most likely this happens through cleaning it, removing every bit of infection, bacteria, fluid, and at times even dead flesh to stop the infection from spreading. As you treat it, the wound begins to heal, and most likely you will have a scar left.

Scars are never pleasant, and they remind us of the past. They are memories of the assault or accident we experienced. Some people will even go to the extent to try to remove the scar because it's the only way to move on in their life entirely.

The infection represents the demonic oppression or possession that has been inflicted either by open doors or attacks of the enemy.

Often, this happens through abuse or traumas we experience in life. The infection (demonic influence) must be removed from the wound to begin to heal. Once it begins to heal, the difference between the natural and spiritual is that God never intended us to have any scars spiritually. The scar represents an incomplete process. The scars represent the memories or trauma, the tendency to revert to certain sins or habits due to lack of inner healing. Inner healing is the process of removing the scar tissue so that we maintain and have long lasting freedom in our life.

When we don't complete the process of deliverance, scars can be sensitive and keep us vulnerable; triggering past events, habits, sins, and ways we never want to revisit. Removing the scar and allowing the wound to heal completely is the key to experiencing complete freedom in Christ. The good news is that Christ has provided a way for us to experience such freedom. Regardless of the reason why you experienced demonic influence in your life, there is a way to evict them and obtain victory of the open door that allowed them to control your life. The key will be in identifying the open door that gave them access and allowing the Holy Spirit to heal and completely restore you!

SCRIPTURAL FOUNDATION FOR INNER HEALING

One of the most common questions about inner healing is whether it's scriptural or not. The term inner healing isn't found in scripture. It is simply a term to describe a way God uses to heal us emotionally and spiritually. An important aspect of inner healing is the knowledge and understanding of how God has designed us. It's because of a lack of knowledge that it has caused us to focus solely on the demonic influence forgetting to complete the process of freedom. We are all a tri-part human—body, soul, and spirit. Our outer man is the human physical body, while our inner man is composed of both soul and spirit.

> "Now may the God of peace himself sanctify you completely, and may your whole spirit and soul and body be kept blameless at the coming of our Lord Jesus Christ. He who calls you is faithful; he will surely do it." (1 Thessalonians 5:23–24, ESV)

Scripture asks us, *"to put off your old self, which belongs to your former manner of life and is corrupt through deceitful desires, and to be renewed in the spirit of your minds, and to put on the new self, created after the likeness of*

God in true righteousness and holiness." (Ephesians 4:22–24, ESV)

The old self is composed of past experiences, sins, habits, traumas that we must put off through healing and restoration for us to bring on the new self, created after the likeness of God! This process requires that we live a daily life of righteousness, but what about when victory over the old-self seems impossible?

BROKENHEARTED | SHABHAR

Scripture talks about the brokenhearted. The Hebrew word for brokenhearted is shabhar, meaning to break, crush, destroy. Sin causes our innocence to be shattered, trauma and abuse cause our memories, identity, and confidence to be shattered. Rejection can hurt and cause our heart to be offended and eventually broken by cycles of hurts. As you can see, the goal of the enemy is to keep us brokenhearted ultimately. Proverbs 17:22 declares that *"A joyful heart is good medicine, but a crushed spirit dries up the bones."*

Inner healing is the process of binding up the broken heart, and it is through His anointing that we are healed and restored. Let me share a personal testimony that can help better understand. Growing up, I was abused verbally and physically. This created in me anger and hate for everyone, including God. This anger and hate turned into rage, provoking outbursts of violence. It was during the years of abuse that a demonic spirit entered my life; it was the physical and verbal abuse that shattered my identity and innocence.

Of course, ultimately it was an assignment of the enemy to keep me broken and eventually destroy my life. When I went through deliverance, I remember that the ministers understood deliverance but lacked an understanding of inner healing.

During my deliverance session, I was free of the outbursts of anger, a measure of healing began to take place as I forgave my abusers. But deep inside I felt a brokenness (scarring) that had not completely healed. The scarring opened the door for continued oppression on and off in my life for many years.

The anger and hate with bursts of violence were replaced with a performance and striving mentality; looking for approval through my works and actions. Now I was left with insecurity and lack of confidence, a broken heart. It was not until many years later, while I was in prayer that I heard God speak to me about my past and healed my heart completely. I remember as if it was yesterday. I was attending bible college; I was in my bedroom while praying I wept because I could finally stop striving for approval. I knew I was loved, accepted, and healed from my broken heart. It was at that time that a boldness was birthed in me. It was because I could receive my identity as His son, the Spirit of Adoption. I felt secure, confident, and loved!

Although in deliverance I had been set free from the oppression of the demonic spirits that caused me to be violent, I had not been healed completely in my heart from the wounds of my past. I needed inner healing, and He made way for me to receive it!

HOW DO I RECEIVE INNER HEALING?

Many great ministries offer inner healing; they use various methods of "prayer counseling" ultimately helping and aiding in obtaining complete deliverance in your life. The purpose of this chapter is to make you aware that there is another explanation as to why you may not have experienced total freedom in your life.

I would like to share with you two biblical principles that will help in obtaining healing of your heart. If you are not successful in getting complete freedom, it's important to always ask for help.

Speak with your Pastor, Mentor or Spiritual Covering. They may have a particular ministry available to assist you in receiving inner healing. The following two principles can help begin the healing process, and some may even need more in-depth ministry to obtain freedom.

KINGDOM PRINCIPLES TO INNER-HEALING

CONFESSION & REPENTANCE

Often we think about confession only when we refer to sin. But confession can be used for releasing traumas, hurts, and pains. In prayer, we can confess to God our fears, our hurts, bringing to light the shattered areas of our life. Confession is not to inform God of our emotional hurts, traumas or problems; it is to render powerless the thoughts, actions, and habits that have built cycles that empower memories, traumas, and pains.

Confession is the way we initiate a supernatural exchange. It is you releasing to God what hurts, hinders, and wounds you in return for His healing, restoration, and wholeness. Often, you will find areas that need repentance during this time, when you encounter areas where you have held unforgiveness or allowed yourself to live in sin because of those hurts, repent.

> "When the righteous cry for help, the Lord hears and delivers them out of all their troubles. The Lord is near to the brokenhearted and saves the crushed in spirit." (Psalm 34:17–18, ESV)

King David often cried out to the Lord, and this was his confession of need and dependence in the fact that only God could deliver him and make him whole. Many times we think of the Psalms as just worship and praise, but they are filled with confessions of troubled hearts and minds.

> "If we confess our sins, He is faithful and just to forgive us our sins and cleanse us from all unrighteousness." (1 John 1:9, MEV)

> "Therefore, repent and be converted, that your sins may be wiped away, that times of refreshing may come from the presence of the Lord, and that He may send the One who previously was preached to you, Jesus Christ," (Acts 3:19–20, MEV)

When I went through inner healing, I would pour out my heart to God. Don't minimize the power of prayer with God. Those moments, where your mind can't focus on anything else but pouring out what troubles you are the key to releasing and rendering powerless the offenses, pains and hurts of your life.

SET YOUR MIND | RENEW YOUR MIND | PUT ON NEW NATURE

After confessing and repenting we must begin to renew our mind and put on the new nature of Christ in our life. One of the most powerful ways to renew our mind and put on the new nature is to set our mind on things above. Read Colossians 3 and practice setting your mind on things above. Let it be renewed and transformed by putting on your new heavenly nature.

> "Therefore, if any man is in Christ, he is a new creature. Old things have passed away. Look, all things have become new." (2 Corinthians 5:17, MEV)

> "Do not be conformed to this world, but be transformed by the renewing of your mind, that you may prove what is the good and acceptable and perfect will of God." (Romans 12:2, MEV)

An important aspect of setting our minds on things above is receiving a revelation of who we are in Christ. Confession and repentance are incomplete without laying a foundation that can keep us stable and rooted in our freedom.

Confession of Scripture is important, but often people have started with confession of scripture, not realizing that there are underlying issues that need to be addressed so the word (seed) can fall in their heart (ground) and be able to take root and blossom.

Confess and declare God's Word into your spirit, mind, and body.

SET YOUR MIND IN YOUR NEW IDENTITY

I AM ACCEPTED...

John 1:12 I am God's Child

John 15:15 I am Christ's Friend.

Romans 5:1 I have been justified.

1 Corinthians 6:17 I am united with the Lord (one spirit).

Corinthians 6:19-20 I am bought with a price; I belong to God.

1 Corinthians 12:27 I am a member of Christ's Body.

Ephesians 1:1 I am a saint.

Col 1:14 I have been redeemed and forgiven.

Col 2:10 I am complete in Christ.

I AM SECURE...

Romans 8:1-2 I am free forever from condemnation.

Romans 8:28 I am assured all works together for good.

Romans 8:31-34 I am free from any charge against me.

Romans 8:35-39 I cannot be separated from the love of God.

Corinthians 1:21-22 I am established, anointed, sealed by God.

Colossians 3:3 I am hidden in Christ in God.

2 Tim 1:7 I have not been given a spirit of fear, but of power, love, and a sound mind.

Hebrews 4:16 I can find grace and mercy in time of need.

John 5:18 I am born of God; the evil one cannot touch me.

I Am Significant...

Matthew 5:13-14 I am the salt and light of the earth.

John 15:1,5 I am a branch of the true vine, a channel of His Life.

John 15:16 I have been chosen and appointed to bear fruit.

Acts 1:8 I am a personal witness of Christ.

1 Corinthians 3:16 I am God's temple.

2 Corinthians 5:17-21 I am a minister of reconciliation for God.

Ephesians 2:6 I am seated with Christ in heavenly realm.

Ephesians 2:10 I am God's workmanship.

Ephesians 3:12 I can approach God with freedom and confidence.

In Conclusion: Inner healing deals with our emotional, soulish, and thought life in ways that help us maintain our freedom long term.

If you have tried deliverance and it has not been effective, most likely you need to find roots that have kept doors open, and sometimes these roots lead us to experiences in life that scarred us, and we need healing.

CHAPTER 4

OPEN DOORS AND COMMON HINDRANCES TO DELIVERANCE

". . . areas in the redeemed life not yielded to God offer open doors to demon powers. They are eager to seize the slightest opportunity to enter the life of those who were once abjectly enslaved to them. For this reason, a person set free from occult bondage must make a clean sweep of any complicity with evil. It is of extreme importance that he withhold nothing in his life from the Lord."

Merrill Frederick Unger

What Demons Can Do to Saints

The devil is a legal expert, He knows the word of God and will try to find every possible way to gain a legal right to your life. He even believes in God and trembles (James 2:19). We must be discerning to recognize the open doors that give the enemy legal access to our lives.

In this chapter, we will review the open doors and most common hindrances to receiving deliverance. Open doors are access points, while hindrances are aspects of legal rights the enemy has over a person. Let's begin by looking at common open doors.

One of those major doors is sin, among many others.

OPEN DOORS

WILLFUL SIN

Colossians 1:12-14 "giving thanks to the Father, who has qualified you to share in the inheritance of the saints in light. He has delivered us from the domain of darkness and transferred us to the kingdom of his beloved Son, in whom we have redemption, the forgiveness of sins".

Sin:
1. Separates us from God
2. Opens doors for the enemy to legally rule us.

BITTERNESS AND UNFORGIVENESS

Matthew 18:34-35"And his master was angry, and delivered him to the torturers until he should pay all that was due to him.35 "So My heavenly Father also will do to you if each of you, from his heart, does not forgive his brother his trespasses."

HURTS AND WOUNDS

Proverbs 18:14 "The spirit of a man will sustain him in sickness, but who can bear a broken spirit?"

VOWS

Exodus 23:32-33 "You shall make no covenant with them, nor with their gods. 33 They shall not dwell in your land, lest they make you sin against Me. For if you serve their gods, it will surely be a snare to you."

Exodus 34:12 "Take heed to yourself, lest you make a covenant with the inhabitants of the land where you are going, lest it be a snare in your midst."

INIQUITY AND CURSES

Exodus 34:7 "keeping mercy for thousands, forgiving iniquity and transgression and sin, by no means clearing the guilty, visiting the iniquity of the fathers upon the children and the children's children to the third and the fourth generation."

Deuteronomy 5:9 "you shall not bow down to them nor serve them. For I, the Lord your God, am a jealous God, visiting the iniquity of the fathers upon the children to the third and fourth generations of those who hate Me,

Iniquity and curses can keep people under bondage and captivity. Many don't even know they are

dealing with it. It gives the enemy an open door to torment and rule over your life.

IDOLS

Exodus 20:3 "You shall have no other gods before Me."

God is a jealous God, and He will not share His Glory with no one or thing. Those with past idolatry, occult practice, either directly or indirectly have open doors in their lives to demonic oppression.

Many of God's prophets spoke out boldly against idolatry. (Isaiah 2:8; Jeremiah 50:2; Ezekiel 6:4-6; Micah 1:7; Habakkuk 2:18; and Zechariah 13:2).

We must ask ourselves "Whom will we serve?" (Joshua 24:15-16). We must be careful not to give the devil any legal access to our life.

COMMON BARRIERS TO DELIVERANCE

If there are any hindrances when it comes to deliverance, it is never on God's side. Some of these obstacles or impediments are more common than others. When ministering deliverance, addressing these seven barriers can bring a breakthrough. These are only seven common ones, but being led by the Spirit can uncover others and help you to minister effectively.

IGNORANCE OF GOD'S WORD AND WILL

This is common in the Church today; Christians do not know the fundamental teachings and basic teachings of the Word of God and His Will.

> "Therefore My people go into captivity because they have no knowledge; and their honorable men are famished, and their multitude dried up with thirst." (Isaiah 5:13, MEV)

> "My people are destroyed for lack of knowledge. Because you have rejected knowledge, I will reject you from being My priest. And because you have forgotten the law of your God, I will also forget your children." (Hosea 4:6, MEV)

We must confess our sin of ignorance: God, I confess I have been ignorant of my fault, I confess it as a sin, and I repent of it. I ask that you forgive me; help me seek your truth. In Jesus' name. Amen.

UNBELIEF

Many of Churches regard unbelief as harmless. The Word of God calls it a sin. This can shift the atmosphere; it can release an atmosphere of faith when we repent of the sin of unbelief.

> "Be attentive, brothers, lest there be in any of you an evil, unbelieving heart, and you depart from the living God." (Hebrews 3:12, MEV)

We must confess our unbelief and confess our faith: *God, we come to you in Jesus' name. I confess my sin of unbelief; I will not excuse it. I am responsible for it.*

I am sorry for it. I ask you to forgive me and to deliver me from it. Impart your faith. I declare I believe in God the

Father; I believe in Jesus Christ His Son; I believe in God the Holy Spirit. I believe in the Word of God. I believe Jesus what you said; God's word is the truth. Amen.

UNCONFESSED SIN

Proverbs 28:13 is a principle. If it is covered and unforgiven sin you will not prosper, hiding sin brings death. Many people think *"If I don't confess my sin to God, He will never know it."* This is a lie of the enemy. The truth is, He does know. He does not ask for you to confess for Him to find out, but to help you.

Take the time to search your heart, let God cleanse you and forgive you. Confess your sin, repent of it and renounce it. Receive His forgiveness and forgive yourself because He has forgiven you.

OCCULT INVOLVEMENT

Occult practices like: fortune telling, horoscopes, Ouija boards, superstitions, black and white magic, occult rock music, drugs, and freemason are barriers to deliverance. It's important when ministering or receiving deliverance to completely expose every practice that can hinder our freedom.

> "You must not bow down to their gods, or serve them, or do according to their practices, but you shall utterly overthrow them and break down their images in pieces. You shall serve the LORD your God, and He shall bless your bread and your water, and I will remove sickness from your midst. No one shall be miscarrying or be barren in your land. I will fulfill the number of your days." (Exodus 23:24–26, MEV)

These are instructions from Moses on how to deal with other religions and evil practices. Idols, even things that you may have obtained as a souvenir or decoration from another country, can bring occult presence and curse over your life.

Ask God to show you anything you have been involved in, even objects you may be in possession at home.

Prayer for Deliverance: *Lord, if I have ever been involved in the occult, even ignorantly, whatever it was, I confess it as a sin. I renounce it, and I ask you to forgive me, I commit myself now that never again I will be involved with those things. Forgive me. Release me from their influence right now in the name of Jesus. Amen.*

COVENANT WITH FALSE GODS OR COVENANT WITH THOSE WHO DO.

Freemasonry. If you are involved in it, you are under a curse. It is an abomination in the sight of God. Secret societies and occult groups are false gods.

> "You must not make a covenant with them or with their gods. They shall not live in your land, lest they cause you to sin against Me, for if you serve their gods, it will surely be a snare to you." (Exodus 23:32–33, MEV)

Prayer of Renunciation: Lord Jesus Christ, I want to serve you and to love you. If there is in my life or my family the curse of Freemasonry or any other cult, I ask you to release me and forgive me; break its power over me right now. In Jesus' name. Amen.

CURSES

The key word for curse is *"frustration."* You are on the verge of success, and something goes wrong. The key is to renounce the cause of curse in your life.

COMMON SYMPTOMS OF A CURSE: FROM DEREK PRINCE

- Mental and Emotional Breakdown. (Depression)
- Repeated and Chronic Sickness.
- Repeated miscarriages and female problems. (tumors)
- Marriage and Family Breakdown.
- Financial Problems (Poverty Syndrome)
- Accident Prone (always having an accident)
- History of Suicide or Unnatural Deaths.

Prayer to Break Curses: *Thank you, Jesus, that on the Cross you were made a curse that I may be redeemed from the curse and enter into the blessing. Because of what you did tonight in your name, I release myself from every curse over my family and me. I claim the blessing that you purchased with your blood. Thank you, Lord Jesus. Amen.*

CHAPTER 5

BLESSINGS DELIVERANCE FROM CURSES

"Every curse that might have come on us came on Jesus instead, that all the blessings due Him might be made available to us. Jesus was actually made a curse in our place, that we might receive "the blessing of Abraham." In what ways was Abraham blessed? Genesis 24:1 reveals the answer: "Abraham was old, well advanced in age; and the Lord had blessed Abraham in all things." The blessing of Abraham, then, covers every area of our lives, and that is the blessing that was made available to us through faith in the exchange that took place when Jesus was made a curse for us on the cross."

Derek Prince

Bought with Blood: The Divine Exchange at the Cross

In the next two chapters, we will look at the power of God's blessing to deliver us from curses and iniquity. First, let me define the difference between a curse and iniquity. For that let's turn to Exodus 34:6-9 & Galatians 3:13-14

> "The LORD passed before him and proclaimed, "The LORD, the LORD, a God merciful and gracious, slow to anger, and abounding in steadfast love and faithfulness, keeping steadfast love for thousands, forgiving iniquity and transgression and sin, but who will by no means clear the guilty, visiting the iniquity of the fathers on the children and the children's children, to the third and the fourth generation." And Moses quickly bowed his head toward the earth and worshiped. And he said, "If now I have found favor in your sight, O Lord, please let the Lord go in the midst of us, for it is a stiff- necked people, and pardon our iniquity and our sin, and take us for your inheritance."" (Exodus 34:6–9, ESV)

> "Christ redeemed us from the curse of the law by becoming a curse for us — for it is written, "Cursed is everyone who is hanged on a tree"— so that in Christ Jesus the blessing of Abraham might come to the Gentiles, so that we might receive the promised Spirit through faith." (Galatians 3:13–14, ESV)

DEFINITIONS

Iniquity – āwōn: the punishment, consequence, recompense for transgressing against God. It comes from the word avon meaning *"a bend, twist or distortion."* In other words, iniquity is a propensity in your family line for certain sins or rebellion against God. Unrepentant sin and disobedience in the bloodlines through our ancestors is the cause of this. (Exodus 34:6-9)

Curse – qĕlālâ: the absence or reversal of blessings or rightful state and lowering to a lesser state. (Deuteronomy 28)

Sin – ḥaṭṭ āʾt: meaning sinful condition, guilty of sin, continually walking in a direction not pleasing to God. (Exodus 34:6-9)

WHAT IS A CURSE?

"A curse is God's recompense in the life of a person and his or her descendants as a result of iniquity. The curse causes sorrow of heart and gives demonic spirits legal entry into a family whereby they can carry out and perpetuate their wicked devices." -Chuck D. Pierce and Rebecca Wagner Systema, Protecting Your Home from Spiritual Darkness

Usually, people who have a curse at operation in their lives say the following thing:

- No matter what I do, I feel like I fail every time I am on the verge of success.
- I feel like everything good happens to everyone else except me. Success eludes me all the time.
- I feel like I am haunted by failure, grief, and death.
- I always deal with this same issue. I pray, I fast, I get deliverance, but it seems always to come back.
- My mom had this, my grandmother did, and now I do!

KEYWORD

Frustration – it is like a shadow that follows you around, harassing you and always oppressing you. Derek Prince says it can be like a long, evil arm stretched out from the past, and it rests upon you with a dark, oppressive force that inhibits the full expression of your personality. You never feel completely free to be yourself. You sense that you have potential within you that is never fully developed. You always expect more of you than you can achieve. This arm grips you, pulls you back, and causes you to stumble.

THE INVISIBLE REALM

Both curses and blessings operate in the invisible realm. They shape the course of history and the lives of people.

In 2 Corinthians 4:17-18, the Apostle Paul says that the visible things are temporary, but the invisible are eternal. Therefore, we must pay attention to the invisible realm more than natural. Both blessings and curses belong to the invisible, spiritual realm. They are vehicles of supernatural, spiritual power.

BLESSINGS | produce good and beneficial results.

CURSES | produce bad and harmful results.

Both curses and blessings are mentioned over 640 times in the word.

HOW CURSES ARE ACTIVATED

(SEE APPENDIX B FOR MORE DETAILS)

One of the primary vehicles of blessings and curses is words; either written or spoken.

> Proverbs 11:9 "The hypocrite with his mouth destroys his neighbor, but through knowledge the righteous will be delivered."

> Proverbs 12:18 "There is one who speaks like the piercing of a sword, but the tongue of the wise promotes health."

> Proverbs 15:4 "A wholesome tongue is a tree of life, but perverseness in it breaks the spirit."

> Proverbs 18:21 "Death and life are in the power of the tongue, and those who love it will eat its fruit."

We do well to heed the warning Jesus gave us in regard to how we will be justified on the day of judgement. Our words have eternal consequences. We must put a guard on our tongue and sanctify our words to release blessings instead of curses.

> ""Either make the tree good and its fruit good, or make the tree bad and its fruit bad, for the tree is known by its fruit. You brood of vipers! How can you speak good, when you are evil? For out of the abundance of the heart the mouth speaks. The good person out of his good treasure brings forth good, and the evil person out of his evil treasure brings forth evil. I tell you, on the day of judgment people will give account for every careless word they speak, for by your words you will be justified, and by your words you will be condemned."" (Matthew 12:33–37, ESV)

SIGNS OF A CURSE

> Deuteronomy 28:15 "But if you will not obey the voice of the Lord your God or be careful to do all his commandments and his statutes

that I command you today, then all these curses shall come upon you and overtake you.

The cause of curses is exactly opposite of blessings. Blessings are a result of hearing God's voice and obeying it. The cause of curses is not hearing God's voice and not doing what He says. While some curses come upon us generationally, we have the power to choose to hear and obey God and break those curses over our life.

SEVEN INDICATIONS OF A CURSE

TAKEN FROM | Derek Prince, Bought with Blood: The Divine Exchange at the Cross

Now I will give you seven indications of a curse, which I have learned by observation in dealing with people, independently of Deuteronomy 28. (But it is remarkable how much they agree!) If you have only one of these problems, it may or may not be a curse. If you have several of them, you may be almost sure you are under a curse.

1.   Mental or emotional breakdown.

2.   Repeated or chronic sickness, especially if it is hereditary, which is the nature of a curse.

3.   Female problems (barrenness, miscarriages, menstrual cramps and a whole host of others). When I minister to the sick, and a woman comes forward with one of these problems, I simply assume it is a curse, and seldom am I wrong. I have a pile of testimonies of women who have been completely set free from these conditions after a curse over their lives was canceled.

4.   Breakdown of marriage or family alienation. Some families just cannot stick together. Husbands and wives divorce, remarry, and often divorce again. Children, too, are alienated from their parents.

5.   Financial insufficiency. Most of us go through times of financial hardship. I am no exception. But if you are always struggling, if you never have enough, that is probably a curse.

6.   Being accident-prone. If you are one of those people to whom accidents always happen—you step off the curb and break your ankle; you are in a car and somebody slams into you—you are probably under a curse.

A characteristic phrase would be, "Why does it always happen to me?"

7.   A history of suicide or unnatural deaths in a family.

BLESSINGS AND CURSES TAKEN FROM | Derek Prince, Bought with Blood

Here are short summaries of the blessings and the curses in Deuteronomy 28. I suggest you read the chapter for yourself and decide whether you agree with my summary. First the blessings:

1.   Personal exaltation. By this I mean being lifted up, honored.

2.   Reproductiveness. I use this word to describe a person who reproduces, or is fruitful, in every area of life, whether physical or financial or relational or creative.

3.   Health. You probably do not appreciate how much of a blessing health is until you are sick, and then you may wish you had thanked God more often for the blessing of being healthy.

4.   Prosperity or success. Prosperity in the Bible does not mean what it does to modern Americans. It is not luxurious living or an abundance of physical pleasures, but accomplishing God's purpose and succeeding in doing His will. In Joshua 1:8, the Lord promised Joshua that whatever he did would prosper and that he would have good success. Yet the leader of the Israelites spent many of the following years in warfare, always exposed to danger, sleeping in open fields and leading the tough life of a soldier in war.

5.   Victory. Blessing brings victory in every conflict that we enter in the will of God.

6.   Being the head and not the tail. Some years ago, I asked the Lord to tell me the difference between the head and the tail. He gave me a simple answer: The head makes the decisions, and the tail gets dragged around. Let me ask you: How you are living—like a head or a tail? Do you make the decisions? Are your plans carried out successfully? Or are you the victim of pressures and forces and circumstances that drag you around, and you do not know what to expect next?

7.   Being above and not beneath. This goes closely with being the head and not the tail.

The curses from Deuteronomy 28 are the opposite of the blessings:

1.   Humiliation.

2.   Failure to reproduce or barrenness (the opposite of reproductiveness). Almost invariably barrenness is the result of a curse.

3.   Sickness of every kind. One category of sickness that is particularly indicative of a curse is one that is called hereditary, continuing on from generation to generation.

4.   Poverty and failure.

5.   Defeat—just the opposite of the blessing of victory.

6.   Being the tail and not the head.

7.   Being beneath and not above.

YOU ARE NOT A VICTIM

Scripture clearly states that God visits the iniquity of fathers upon the children up to the third and fourth generation (Exodus 20:5).

Curses pop-up, but not without a cause. Someone gives them legal right to visit the family line. Willful disobedience or lack of revelation can be the activating point of a curse.

> "The LORD's curse is on the house of the wicked, but he blesses the dwelling of the righteous. Toward the scorners he is scornful, but to the humble he gives favor." (Proverbs 3:33–34, ESV)

When we live under curses for extended periods of time, we can develop a victim mentality that traps us in a cycle of self-pity. I want to declare to you that "You're not a Victim!" You're a candidate, ready to experience a depth of freedom promised by your Heavenly Father.

Pray this prayer with me.

Heavenly Father, I thank you that you have made a way through your Son Jesus for me to be free from curses. I ask that you give me the grace to humble myself before you and receive my freedom. In Jesus' name. Amen!

BREAKING FREE FROM CURSES

We are citizens of the Kingdom of God, and we have spiritual authority and power over curses. We can determine what we are coming against by learning to discern and understand how curses operate. It's the revelation of Christ's divine exchange on the Cross that gives us the power and authority to be free from curses in our life.

> "Christ redeemed us from the curse of the law by becoming a curse for us — for it is written, "Cursed is everyone who is hanged on a tree"— so that in Christ Jesus the blessing of Abraham might come to the Gentiles, so that we might receive the promised Spirit through faith." (Galatians 3:13–14, ESV)

77

REDEEMED | SECURED RELEASE & DELIVERANCE

The verb translated redeemed (literally, "to buy up") has here the primary meaning of "to effect deliverance" or "to secure the release of someone," at some cost to the person who secures it in terms of effort, suffering, or loss. - UBS Handbook on Letter to Galatians

Jesus has secured our freedom through His death and resurrection. When Jesus hung on the cross, He became the curse so we would not live under the consequences of a curse. The key to being set free from curses is to appropriate ourselves of this divine exchange that has taken place. How do we receive this divine exchange as our own?

IDENTIFY

Through prayer, led by the Holy Spirit with the list above identify the potential curse you may be confronting.

IDENTIFICATIONAL REPENTANCE & FORGIVENESS

IR does not excuse our ancestors from giving an account to God for their sins. It only cuts the influence of the right the curse has had generationally over your life. If you have knowledge of your ancestors' lifestyle or history, you may realize that there was a generational sin that opened the door for this curse.

Repeat a simple prayer as *"Heavenly Father; I repent of the sins of my ancestors. I forgive my ancestors, back three and four generations for causing sin to enter my life bloodline. I cut off the influence of their sins and their legal rights into my life and family. In Jesus' name. Amen.*

PERSONAL REPENTANCE

When a curse has activated because of personal sin, rebellion or disobedience. It's important to confess and repent before God. Pray "Heavenly Father, I confess (sin, rebellion, etc...) and I repent for it, I renounce the works of the enemy. In Jesus' name. Amen.

APPROPRIATE YOURSELF OF HIS BLESSING

After identifying the cause of the curse and appropriately repenting generationally and personally, we now move onto releasing blessings. The way we appropriate ourselves of the blessings Christ has promised for us is through faith. The Apostle Paul revealed to us the reason why Christ became a curse for us: *"so that in Christ Jesus the blessing of Abraham might come to the Gentiles, so that we might receive the promised Spirit through faith."* (Galatians 3:14, ESV) Often, when you have repented a sense of clarity will come to your mind, heart, and spirit. It is at this time you will sense like the invisible forces that gripped you for years no longer have influence or power. At this time, activate the blessing through faith. I recommend you make a list of declarations from Deuteronomy 28 and confess, declare in faith those blessings over your life.

WHAT TO DO WHEN YOU DON'T SEE RESULTS

"I tried, and nothing happened!" Voices of discouragement will speak, and the best course of action is to ask for help. Experienced ministers will be able to pray and discern if something is missing in the process you have been walking towards freedom. Sometimes, an experienced minister carries a measure of anointing that can release the breakthrough for your life. Don't give up; the very fact you have a desire to be free reveals that you have the right heart, and God is ready to release you from the oppression of curses.

CHAPTER 6

BLESSINGS DELIVERANCE FROM INIQUITY

"Difficult as it may be to understand in a society as individualistic as our own, the sins of our forefathers and foremothers can greatly affect who we are today, what spiritual challenges we face, and what sins we may be most susceptible to. Perhaps the easiest analogy we have for understanding how this occurs is through our knowledge of genetics. Just as we may inherit our mother's nose or our father's eyes, we may also inherit our mother's legalism or our father's alcoholism. Unrepentant sin can leave a spiritual weakness toward that sin in a family line (called iniquity) just as diabetes can leave a physical weakness toward diabetes in a family line. The definition of sin is missing the mark or breaking the law of God. The definition of iniquity is a generational deviation from God's proper path. Because of sin in the generations, the iniquity of that sin can be passed on to the children."

Chuck D. Pierce and Rebecca Wagner Sytsema

Possessing Your Inheritance: Take Hold of God's Destiny for Your Life, Second Edition.

DELIVERANCE AND INNER HEALING

WHAT IS INIQUITY?

The Apostle Paul referred to iniquity as a mystery. After doing a word study of the original words used for iniquity, we can gain a better understanding of what Iniquity is. The word iniquity is the word awon. It means iniquity, guilt, or punishment for guilt. The root word from which this one comes is "to err, to go astray." It gives us the idea of deviating from the right path.

Iniquity also gives us the idea of generational wickedness (sinfulness). A generation is usually a period of about 30 to 40 years. When we look at the history of a generation, we can find patterns of righteousness or iniquity. Consequently, God visits the "iniquity of the fathers on the children to the third and fourth generation..." (Exodus 20:5)

The Bible says that God hates iniquity. Hebrews 1:9 states, "You have loved righteousness and hated lawlessness (iniquity); Therefore God, Your God, has anointed you with the oil of gladness more than your companions."

Lawlessness and wickedness, are two other ways to translate iniquity. The root word of iniquity in the Greek means "injustice, without law, and no regard for the rule of law."

Iniquity is ultimately something that leads to a lifestyle outside of God's rulership, and it is something that causes us to go astray and into error. It is something that is passed down from one generation to another. God desires to cleanse us from all iniquity and to rid our family bloodline of iniquitous patterns.

"Then he showed me Joshua the high priest standing before the angel of the Lord, and Satan standing at his right hand to accuse him. And the Lord said to Satan, "The Lord rebuke you, O Satan! The Lord who has chosen Jerusalem rebuke you! Is not this a brand plucked from the fire?" Now Joshua was standing before the angel, clothed with filthy garments. And the angel said to those who were standing before him, "Remove the filthy garments from him." And to him he said, "Behold, I have taken your iniquity away from you, and I will clothe you with pure vestments." And I said, "Let them put a clean turban on his head." So they put a clean turban on his head and clothed him with garments. And the angel of the Lord was standing by." (Zechariah 3:1–5, ESV)

When Satan, filled his heart with iniquity, God cast him out of the Heavens into the earth. It was at this precise time that for the first time, the earth experienced the consequences of iniquity, through lawlessness, rebellion, and perversion. Ezekiel 28:15-16 "

You were perfect in your ways from the day you were created, till iniquity was found in you. 16 "By the abundance of your trading You became filled with violence within, and you sinned; Therefore I cast you as a profane thing Out of the mountain of God; And I destroyed you, O covering cherub, From the midst of the fiery stones.

At the Garden of Eden, in God's perfect presence, in a perfect relationship, Adam and Eve for the first time were presented with the choice to go astray from the path God had laid out. When they chose to disobey God, iniquity entered the bloodline of humanity. Men began to twist and distort everything God had given to him. Psalm 51:5 reveals to us that every child born after original sin was bound to be born into iniquity. Behold, I was brought forth in iniquity, and in sin my mother conceived me. (Psalm 51:5)

Every human being is born with iniquity or law-lessness in their heart. Iniquity can be passed down from generation to generation.

Remember Exodus 34 says, *"visiting the iniquity of the fathers on the children and the children's children, to the third and the fourth generation."*

Jeremiah 17 gives us a picture of the power of iniquity and sin. Jeremiah prophesies that sin is "written with a pen of iron; with a point of a diamond it is engraved on the tablet of their heart, and on the horns of their altars..." He goes on to prophesy the destruction and loss they will experience because of their wickedness. Ultimately, iniquity cannot be resolved by our works. Jeremiah prophesied to Judah saying, "Cursed is the man who trusts in man and makes flesh his strength, whose heart turns away from the Lord." But in the same prophecy, He gives them hope of faith in God's power to deliver them. Blessed is the man who trusts in the LORD, whose trust is the LORD. 8 He is like a tree planted by water, that sends out its roots by the stream, and does not fear when heat comes, for its leaves remain green, and is not anxious in the year of drought, for it does not cease to bear fruit."

Iniquity acts as an instrument that pulls all things evil, sinful, unjust, and perverse. Very often, people who are living with the consequences of iniquity in their life experience constant sickness, poverty, or depression. These are only three of the common effects of iniquity.

THE IMPORTANCE OF NOT IGNORING INIQUITY

Iniquitous patterns find their way through family bloodlines by legal right. It searches for doors that give it access, and legal right to do its destructive work. Each believer, just as they visit the doctor and fill out a questionnaire that helps the doctor see if there are any family history of sickness or disease, should take stock of their family history. Not to revisit past sin or traumas, but to effectively bring deliverance to them and their future generations.

As believers, we've asked God for the forgiveness of our sins. After salvation, we expect that all the benefits of freedom and deliverance manifest automatically. After all, that is what the preacher said! The moment we experienced the powerful regenerative work of the cross, we entered into a covenant with God that must be established not only personally, but even generationally as we take on the role of priests in our family line. Many believers who have asked forgiveness for their sins, but have not confessed nor asked for forgiveness of their generational iniquities. Ignoring iniquity keeps oppression only at arm's length. We can see this in my believers who even after powerful encounters can continue to experience the same sins and habits as their past.

OUR TONGUE: HOW INIQUITY IS ACTIVATED.

Scripture declares that the power of life and death is in our tongue. We should not be suprised that it is the primary way that iniquity is activated.

James 3:6 "And the tongue is a fire, a world of iniquity: so is the tongue among our members, that it defileth the whole body, and setteth on fire the course of nature; and it is set on fire of hell." (Job 6:30)

SINK HOLES OF INIQUITY

Psalm 7:14-16 "Behold, he travaileth with iniquity, and hath conceived mischief, and brought forth falsehood. 15 He made a pit, and digged it, and is fallen into the ditch which he made. 16His mischief shall return upon his own head, and his violent dealing shall come down upon his own pate."

INIQUITY CAUSES SICKNESS

Psalm 109:14-18 "May the iniquity of his fathers be remembered before the LORD, and let not the sin of his mother be blotted out! 15 Let them be before the LORD continually, that he may cut off the memory of them from the earth!16 For he did not remember to show kindness, but pursued the poor and needy and the brokenhearted, to put them to death. 17 He loved to curse; let curses come upon him! He did not delight in blessing; may it be far from him! 18 He clothed himself with cursing as his coat; may it soak into his body like water, like oil into his bones!"

Iniquity is so powerful it will penetrate the bones and consequently will bring many infirmities.

INIQUITY CAUSES SEPARATION BETWEEN US AND GOD!

Isaiah 59:2 "but your iniquities have made a separation between you and your God, and your sins have hidden his face from you so that he does not hear."

Gossip, , slander, murmuring, and iniquity will cause you to isolate.

INIQUITY CAUSES JESUS TO SEPARATE HIMSELF FROM US.

Matthew 7:21-23 "Not everyone who says to me, 'Lord, Lord,' will enter the kingdom of heaven, but the one who does the will of my Father who is in heaven. 22 On that day many will say to me, 'Lord, Lord, did we not prophesy in your name, and cast out demons in your name, and do many mighty works in your name?' 23 And then will I declare to them, 'I never knew you; depart from me, you workers of (INIQUITY) lawlessness.'"

The supernatural manifestation of God's anointing, miracles or gifts is not a way to determine if a person is living right before God. A great resource to do an in-depth study on why God works supernaturally through people even though they live in sin is, Dr. Bill Hamon's book, "How Can This Be?" Many believers and even ministers can cast out demons, prophesy, and do miracles, but it does not mean they are doing the will of God. What did Jesus mean by this warning?

"I never knew you" – You never had an encounter with me.

"Depart from me" – You rejected me, rebelled against me, you cannot partake with me. Because of your iniquity.

"Workers of Iniquity" – You never allowed me to rule your life.

In other words, Jesus was saying: "You call me Lord, but you live as you wish, you prophesy, you heal the sick, prophesy and cast out demons, but you do it as you wish and however you want with whomever. You live a life of lawlessness. You did not honor me, you used me."

> Job 15:16 – "How much more abominable and filthy is man, which drinketh iniquity like water?"

COLD LOVE AND HARD HEARTS | INIQUITY

> Matthew 24:12 "And because iniquity shall abound, the love of many shall wax cold."

It is not uncommon for people to turn back to their old ways of living. At times, even long time believers turn away from their faith in Christ. Often, because of their sinfulness and sometimes because of the iniquity of others. We place an unrealistic standard as believers, expecting perfection, not knowing that some may still be dealing with iniquity in their life. When we see a believer sin, steal, give bad testimony of their faith or offended, the love of some grows cold.

BREAKING FREE FROM INIQUITY

IDENTIFY

Through prayer, led by the Holy Spirit, and with the list, above identify the potential iniquitous pattern you may be confronting.

IDENTIFICATIONAL REPENTANCE & FORGIVENESS

IR does not excuse our ancestors from giving an account to God for their sins. It only cuts the influence of the right the iniquity has had generationally over your life. If you have knowledge of your ancestor's lifestyle or history. You may realize that there was a generational sin that opened the door for this iniquity. Repent a simple prayer as "Heavenly Father; I repent for the sins of my ancestors. I forgive them for causing this iniquitous pattern to come into our bloodline. I cut off the influence of their sins and their legal rights into my life and family. In Jesus' name. Amen."

PERSONAL REPENTANCE

If an iniquitous pattern has been activated due to personal sin, rebellion, or disobedience. It's important to confess and repent before God. Pray "Heavenly Father, I confess (sin, rebellion, etc...) and I repent for it, I renounce the works of the enemy. In Jesus' name. Amen."

APPROPRIATE YOURSELF OF HIS BLESSING & MERCY

After identifying the cause of the iniquity and appropriately repenting generationally and personally, we now move onto releasing blessings. The way we appropriate ourselves of the blessings Christ has promised for us is through faith. Hebrews 8:12 declares: *"For I will be merciful toward their iniquities, and I will remember their sins no more."* (Hebrews 8:12, ESV)

WHAT TO DO WHEN YOU DON'T SEE RESULTS

"I tried, and nothing happened!" This is the voice of discouragement, and the best course of action is to ask for help. Experienced ministers will be able to pray and discern if something is missing. Sometimes, an experienced minister carries a measure of anointing that can release the breakthrough for your life. Don't give up, the very fact you have a desire to be free reveals that you have the right heart and God is ready to release you from the oppression of curses.

CHAPTER 7

WORSHIP

"Some people only want to worship, and others only want to be warriors. Both praise and war are necessary. War should come out of worship."

Chuck D. Pierce and John Dickson

The Worship Warrior: Ascending in Worship, Descending in War

"Through the praise of children and infants you have established a stronghold against your enemies, to silence the foe and the avenger." (Psalm 8:2, NIV)

Our praise and worship establish a stronghold of protection against the enemy. Strongholds have one purpose, to protect against attacks from the enemy and his forces. Our praise and worship functions as a shield around our families, homes, and churches.

In spiritual warfare and especially in deliverance, a lifestyle of prayer is necessary to be able to minister deliverance and walk in freedom effectively. One of the secret weapons we have in our arsenal is the weapon of worship and praise.

Unfortunately, not everyone enjoys the pleasure and benefits of it. There are three primary reasons why people don't experience the level of worship and praise that builds such a stronghold around their life:

FEAR | TRADITION | LACK OF KNOWLEDGE

Fear is manifested by self- consciousness. We fear what people will think or say if we shout, clap or dance before God's presence. The antidote to fear is love and love is manifested and revealed to us in times of intimate praise and worship to our God.

Tradition manifests by a sense of devotion to systems that have been passed down from generation to generation as solemn ways of worshipping God. This is the manifestation of a religious spirit. Often speaking to us and saying, "I don't need to shout for God to know I worship Him and Praise Him!" or "God knows that in my heart I worship him and praise him." Scripture clearly says Clap your hands, all peoples! Shout to God with loud songs of joy!" (Psalm 47:1, ESV)

Lack of Knowledge is simply a lack of revelation of the power of our praise and worship. At the same time, lack of knowledge will cause us to criticize and oppose what we don't understand.

> "Blessed be the LORD my strength, who prepares my hands for war, and my fingers to fight; my goodness, and my fortress; my high tower, and my deliverer, my shield, and in whom I trust; who subdues nations under me." (Psalm 144:1-2, MEV)

WHAT IS PRAISE & WORSHIP?

Praise celebrates and honors who God is, while worship honors and celebrates what God has done. Worship and praise is a celebration of the worthiness of God, and it is giving honor to Him because of what He has done and accomplished and what He will do and accomplish!

Worship and praise begin, with focus and recognition of Him. It is in worship and praise that God's presence is established in our midst and released here on earth. When our focus, our praise, and worship is released, Heaven gains access to us here on earth as in heaven.

> "Yet you are holy, enthroned on the praises of Israel." (Psalm 22:3, ESV)

PRAISE & WORSHIP AND DELIVERANCE

When the Spirit of God left Saul, an evil spirit entered into his life. When we live in rebellion and disobedience as Saul did, it opens the door to demonic oppression. It's interesting that Saul's servants knew what to do. They counseled him to "seek out a man who is skillful in playing the lyre, and when the harmful spirit from God is upon you, he will play it, and you will be well."

Saul ordered his servants to look for such a person. One of his servants knew a person that fit the criteria for the task. This person was David, who was known for his worship. The servant said, "I have seen..." this means that he had experienced David's worship ministry at some point. His description of David gives us a glimpse into the transformative power of worship, and it was because David had a lifestyle of worship that he had become famed for it. The servant describes David as, "skillful in playing, a man of valor, a man of war, prudent in speech, and a man of good presence, and the LORD is with him."

One of the ways we are conformed into God's likeness and nature is through Praise and Worship, and it transforms us from the inside out. David carried such a presence of God with Him that scripture says it was "the Lord...with him". Of course, when David would play, it was not just an instrument to him. It was a way to allow God, to be enthroned wherever he went. Of course, Saul loved David because of his ability to bring freedom in times of torment.

But ultimately praise and worship are not just ways to relieve torment and oppression; it is the means by which we create an atmosphere where freedom can reign.

In conclusion, our praise and worship is:

1. A way we build a shield and a stronghold against our enemy.
2. A way we can silence our enemies.
3. A way we can create a Heavenly atmosphere where God can rule and reign in freedom.

POWER OF OUR PRAISE & WORSHIP

- *BLESSINGS*

"If you worship me, the LORD your God, I will bless you with food and water and take away all your illnesses. In your land, no woman will have a miscarriage or be without children. I will give you long lives." (Exodus 23:25–26, GNB)

- *GUIDANCE*

"While they were worshiping the Lord and fasting, the Holy Spirit said, "Set apart for me Barnabas and Saul for the work to which I have called them." Then after fasting and praying they laid their hands on them and sent them off." (Acts 13:2–3, ESV)

- *DELIVERANCE*

"About midnight Paul and Silas were praying and singing hymns to God, and the prisoners were listening to them, and suddenly there was a great earthquake, so that the foundations of the prison were shaken. And immediately all the doors were opened, and everyone's bonds were unfastened." (Acts 16:25–26, ESV)

- *JOY*

"And they worshiped him and returned to Jerusalem with great joy." (Luke 24:52, ESV)

• *A SENSE OF GOD'S PRESENCE*

"And it was the primary duty of the trumpeters and singers to make themselves heard with one voice, to praise and give thanks to Yahweh. And when a sound from the trumpets, cymbals, and other instruments of song was raised to Yahweh—for he is good, because his loyal love is everlasting—then the house, the house of Yahweh, was filled with a cloud. And the priests were not able to stand to minister because of the cloud, for the glory of Yahweh filled the house of God." (2 Chronicles 5:13– 14, LEB)

• *A DEEPER SENSE OF THE LORDSHIP OF CHRIST*

"Therefore God has highly exalted him and bestowed on him the name that is above every name, so that at the name of Jesus every knee should bow, in heaven and on earth and under the earth, and every tongue confess that Jesus Christ is Lord, to the glory of God the Father." (Philippians 2:9–11, ESV)

CHAPTER 8

SELF-DELIVERANCE

"The question is often asked of me, 'Can a person deliver himself of demons?' My answer is 'Yes,' and it is my conviction that a person cannot really keep himself free of demons until he is walking in this dimension of deliverance. How is it that a person can deliver himself? As a believer (and that is our assumption), he has the same authority as the believer that is moving in deliverance ministry. He has the authority in the name of Jesus! And Jesus plainly promised them that believe: 'In my name shall they cast out devils.' (Mark 16:17). Usually a person needs only to learn how to go about self-deliverance. After a person has experienced an initial deliverance at the hands of an experienced minister he can begin to practice self-deliverance."

John Eckhardt

Deliverance and Spiritual Warfare Manual (Lake Mary, FL: Charisma House, 2014), 33.

Self-Deliverance is the exercise of our authority to maintain freedom. In this brief chapter, I will give you steps and prayers to help you continue on the path of liberty.

While some receive deliverance immediately, some walk through a path of progressive deliverance. As believers and ministers of the Kingdom of God, we have to be sensitive to God's process for each. We cannot make one experience a standard for all.

One of the areas of sensitivities (discernment) we need to develop is the extent of bondage a person has in their life. Some are unable to recognize the severity of the bondages they carry. Others believe they are not under any bondage, or completely ignore the possibility that the enemy could be behind some of their issues. Delay is inevitable when we ignore this reality, and they are unable to discern the extent and depth of oppression influence of the demonic in their life.

UNDERSTANDING SPIRITUAL BONDAGE

Spiritual bondage is the influence of demonic spirits that prevent a person from living righteously before God. Often, they know they should be living in holiness, but they are unable to. Spiritual bondage is common in individuals who have areas of their life that are unsubmitted to the Lordship of Jesus Christ.

Some individuals struggle in certain areas like gossip or immorality.

Those areas where Christ's dominion has not been established have become areas of bondage. Spiritual bondages develop over time, they come in subtle ways, and they only become stronger the more they stay hidden in your life.

> Proverbs 28:13 (ESV) says, "Whoever conceals his transgressions will not prosper, but he who confesses and forsakes them will obtain mercy." The New Living Translation says it this way, "People who conceal their sins will not prosper, but if they confess and turn from them, they will receive mercy."

A WORD OF CAUTION:

Self-Deliverance can never replace the kingdom principles of confession and ministry from other believers.
James 5:15-16 says,

> "And the prayer of faith will save the one who is sick, and the Lord will raise him up. And if he has committed sins, he will be forgiven. 16 Therefore, confess your sins to one another and pray for one another, that you may be healed. The prayer of a righteous person has great power as it is working."

James shares with us a powerful truth; prayer is not just for healing physical conditions, but also to heal you of sin conditions. Many, well- intentioned Christians fight on their own in hopes of obtaining victory from sin, not realizing that scriptures give us a clear and indispensable path to victory. Confession is not exposing or revealing your sin; it is to heal you, restore you, and help you overcome.
Dr. Bill Hamon says,

> "If you have had a particular problem for a while and it has been manifested more than three times, I believe it has gone beyond the seed stage and has now sprouted. So it must be dealt with immedi-

ately before its root system becomes intertwined with your personality and performance." (Prophets Pitfalls and Principles Chapter 2)

When we continually allow bad habits, sins, and wrong attitudes to rule our life, we are in danger of them becoming part of our personality, and limiting our success. To be restored, we need others to help us uproot those seeds that create spiritual bondage.

God has given us authority. Through His Holy Spirit we can fight and maintain freedom in our life. Self-Deliverance plays a significant role in this goal.

SELF-DELIVERANCE AND WHY IT MAY NOT WORK?

Self-Deliverance is believers exercising their authority to repent, renounce, forgive, and be forgiven to obtain freedom from spiritual bondage. Common reasons why self-deliverance may not work are, but not limited to:

1. LACK OF REVELATION - A revelation and foundation need to be laid on the authority of the believer and the ministry of deliverance.
2. UNDERESTIMATING THE LEVEL OF SPIRITUAL BONDAGE – I do recommend that a person who has tried on their own to receive deliverance to look for a more experienced minister.
3. INIQUITOUS PATTERNS THAT HAVE BUILT STRENGTH OVER MANY GENERATIONS- In-depth ministry may be needed to uproot and peel away the bondage that has developed over many years.

WHY YOU CAN BENEFIT FROM SELF-ELIVERANCE

The foundation to benefit from Self-Deliverance is a strong faith that it is your inheritance from God as His child. I would like to say that ministers, leaders, pastors, and believers can benefit when there is no one near them to minister to them.

I encourage Pastors to teach their congregation the important revelation of deliverance and that they add to it the understanding that they can exercise their spiritual authority through self- deliverance. It will help save you, hours of counseling, ministry, and prayer for them. Empower them to walk in freedom! (Luke 10:19, ESV)

STEPS TO SELF-DELIVERANCE

IDENTIFY AREAS THAT NEED FREEDOM

The first step in deliverance is to identify areas where deliverance is needed. Write down every sin and spiritual problem that you need deliverance from. Sometimes it's helpful to make a list of things you always struggle with:

Lust, rejection, lying, unforgiveness, fear, anger, generational curses (identify and specify), sickness, depression, passivity, unbelief, pills, alcohol, cigarettes, drugs, pornography, homosexuality, lesbianism, anxiety, loneliness, cancer, sterile, occult

This list is not meant to cover everything. These are just a few examples of some of the areas an individual may be seeking freedom in.

I helpful way to identify areas where ministry is needed is to examine your emotional, moral (sexually, thought, attitudes, will), spiritual, and physical life. Examine every area of your life.

REPENT & RENOUNCE

Once you have made a list, begin to repent and renounce each sin on the list.

USE THIS SAMPLE PRAYER: *I confess that Jesus is my Lord and Savior. I voluntarily renounce every activity of Satan that has been in my life through iniquity, transgression, or sin in my parents, grandparents, ancestors, and me.*

I repent of thoughts, words, and actions consciously and unconsciously that have dishonored Jesus; and I ask forgiveness. I ask you, Lord Jesus, to cleanse me, wash me completely and set me free.

Jesus, I renounce Satan, his demons and all his works, influences, bondages, oppressions, curses, and sicknesses that are in my life. I renounce to all demonic oppressions that separate me from you and prevent me from walking with you. I ask that you do a complete deliverance in me. I believe in your death and resurrection, and from it, my freedom comes. Lord Jesus, I ask you to become my absolute Lord over my life. Amen!

USE YOUR AUTHORITY TO CAST OUT EVERY INTRUDER

After doing this, now proceed to command, order and cast out every demon:

USE THIS SAMPLE PRAYER *"I order every spirit of lust, gossip, slander, etc... (name each one) to come out of my emotions, body, mind, and soul. I order you right now to let go of my body, mind, emotions, and soul, right now in the name of Jesus! Amen"*

Sometimes, you may have specific things the Holy Spirit reveals to you. In that case pray the following way: Spirit of rejection, I bind you and order you in the name of Jesus to come out; I break your power and declare in the name of Jesus I am free, right now! Amen!

Do this, one spirit at a time. Repent, renounce, bind and cast it out in the name of Jesus.

BE FILLED & RESTORED

The last step in self-deliverance is to believe for the Holy Spirit to fill you, refresh you, and renew you. He will heal any areas of brokenness and restore your life to wholeness again!

IMPORTANT PRACTICAL WISDOM & INSTRUCTIONS FOR SELF- DELIVERANCE

- Don't talk to demons. Don't get distracted.
- Do it in private, if you need assistance, seek help from someone with experience.
- You may feel like crying, coughing, throwing up. Trust the Holy Spirit. Work with the Holy Spirit.
- Sometimes breathing out deliberately in faith or coughing is necessary.

- If you did self-deliverance and still feel oppressions, do it again. Maybe there is a particular area you feel you need freedom in still.
- Believe and claim your freedom!
- Through the cross, through the Blood, and in the name of Jesus Christ!
- Be patient; some spiritual bondages take time and revelation from the Holy Spirit to be torn down.

APPENDIX A

SPIRITS MENTIONED IN SCRIPTURE

We find that as Jesus ministered deliverance, there were times that He encountered legions of demons. One account of this is told in the Gospel of Mark 5:9 and Luke 8:30, "And Jesus asked him, 'What is your name?' He replied, 'My name is Legion, for we are many.'" From these two scriptures, we can see that many demons can operate or influence the life of one person.

In this case, they identified themselves as a "legion"; this was a military term used in Rome to mean a division of the Roman Army, usually comprising of 3000 to 6000 soldiers.

The question then comes up, are there particular spirits or demons mentioned in the scripture? A thorough reading of scripture can help us identify if there are or not. I'm thankful for technology because it has allowed me to do this almost at the click of a button.

I have been able to identify over 20 specific evil spirits or demons. It does not mean there are only 20 or so, but scripture gives us a glimpse into the work of evil spirits.

For example, Ephesians 6:12 gives us a look into the hierarchy of the spiritual world, "For we do not wrestle against flesh and blood, but against the rulers, against the authorities, against the cosmic powers over this present darkness, against the spiritual forces of evil in the heavenly places." (NKJV - Says "wickedness")

We see the Apostle Paul, apparently, presents a hierarchy of demonic forces at work.

DELIVERANCE WAS CENTRAL TO THE MINISTRY OF JESUS:

Matthew 4:24 "So his fame spread throughout all Syria, and they brought him all the sick, those afflicted with various diseases and pains, those oppressed by demons, epileptics, and paralytics, and he healed them."

Matthew 8:6 "That evening they brought to him many who were oppressed by demons, and he cast out the spirits with a word and healed all who were sick."

Mark 1:34 "And he healed many who were sick with various diseases, and cast out many demons. And he would not permit the demons to speak, because they knew him."

DELIVERANCE WAS PART OF JESUS' ASSIGNMENT TO THE TWELVE DISCIPLES:

Luke 9:1 "And he called the twelve together and gave them power and authority over all demons and to cure diseases, 2 and he sent them out..."

AND EVEN THE SEVENTY SENT OUT BY JESUS SAW DEMONS OBEY THEM:

Luke 10:1;9;17 "After this the Lord appointed seventy-two others and sent them on ahead of him, two by two, into every town and place where he himself was about to go. Heal the sick in it and say to them, 'The kingdom of God has come near to you.' The seventy-two returned with joy, saying, "Lord, even the demons are subject to us in your name!"

DELIVERANCE IS PART OF THE GREAT COMMISSION ASSIGNED TO ALL BELIEVERS:

Mark 16:15-18 "And he said to them, "Go into all the world and proclaim the gospel to the whole creation. 16 Whoever believes and is baptized will be saved, but whoever does not believe will be condemned. 17 And these signs will accompany those who believe: in my name they will cast out demons; they will speak in new tongues; 18 they will pick up serpents with their hands; and if they drink any deadly poison, it will not hurt them; they will lay their hands on the sick, and they will recover."

Now let's take a look, at the spirits identified in the scriptures:

WICKED SPIRITS

> Ephesians 6:12 For we do not wrestle against flesh and blood, but against the rulers, against the authorities, against the cosmic powers over this present darkness, against the spiritual forces of evil in the heavenly places. (NKJV - Says "wickedness")

Wickedness - poneria - depravity, iniquity (lawlessness), malice, evil purposes, and desires. This word comes from the root word poneros meaning "full of labor, annoyances, hardships, pressed and harassed. These spirits of wickedness are set against you for evil intentions, to cause pain and troubles in your life, with malicious purpose to cause lawlessness to rule in your life.

SPIRIT OF JEZEBEL

In 1 King 18:4 we read about a woman named Jezebel who attacked and killed many of the prophets of God. What is interesting is, that we find her again in the New Testament. In Revelation 2:20 it says,

> "...because you allow that woman Jezebel, who calls herself a prophetess, to teach and seduce My servants to commit sexual immorality and eat things sacrificed to idols. And I gave her time to repent of her sexual immorality, and she did not repent. Indeed I will cast her into a sickbed, and those who commit adultery with her into great tribulation, unless they repent of their deeds. I will kill her children with death, and all the churches shall know that I am He who searches the minds and hearts. And I will give to each one of you according to your works."

It's obvious that is not the same woman that we read of in the Old Testament, but this is the same spirit of Jezebel that operated through her operating today.

This spirit is looking for position and control, in the end seeking to have power. She hates the Apostles and Prophets, if she cannot control and have their position, she will kill them. This demonic spirit kills anything that sounds, smells or looks like the prophetic ministry.

WOUNDED SPIRIT

Proverbs 18:14 says, "The spirit of a man will sustain him in sickness, But who can bear a broken spirit?"

In ministering to many, I have found that those with a wounded spirit can easily be gripped with demonic influences of victimization and self-pity. These spirits come and speak lies to their minds, making them believe that they will never overcome and will never be able to be healed of their hurts and wounds. These wounds are deep and can sometimes be caused by rejection, abuse or any painful and traumatic event.

SPIRIT OF OPPRESSION

Acts 10:28 says that, "...God anointed Jesus of Nazareth with the Holy Spirit and with power. He went about doing good and healing all who were oppressed by the devil, for God was with him."

When people are under the oppression of spirits, things weigh heavy on their mind, they are distressed and feel overpowered by things, these spirits subdue them and at points feel crushed by the troubles that come from every side.

SPIRIT OF SLAVERY (BONDAGE)

> Romans 8:15 says, "For you did not receive the spirit of slavery to fall back into fear, but you have received the Spirit of adoption as sons, by whom we cry, "Abba! Father!"

In the Greek, this is the word doulein, which is related to the word slaves. In the sense of fearing the wrath of its master. God has not given us a spirit of slavery so we should fear Him, rather the Spirit of adoption as sons. We have nothing to fear in Him.

Another manifestation of the spirit of slavery is slaves are subject to the will of another. Many are enslaved to the spirit of bondage and slavery, addictions, etc...

SORROWFUL SPIRIT

> Proverbs 15:13 says, "A glad heart makes a cheerful face, but by sorrow of heart the spirit is crushed."

> 1 Samuel 1:10 says, "She was deeply distressed and prayed to the LORD and wept bitterly."

As I have ministered deliverance, I have discerned that many people at times are under a dark uncontrollable spirit of sorrow that they have succumbed to because of traumatic events in their life. I remember mainly ministering to a young man when I commanded the spirit of sorrow to let go of him, he started weeping and got into a fetal position. After the deliverance was done, he shared about the many years of oppression he had dealt with because of a broken relationship in his family.

SPIRIT OF FEAR

2 Timothy 1:7 says, "for God gave us a spirit not of fear but of power and love and self-control."

Fear will always paralyze you and make your life inactive. I was delivered of a spirit of fear, I would not be able to share the Gospel with boldness until I was delivered from it. Fear attacks your faith, and it causes you to make irrational decisions. Fear can manifest in many different ways:
- Fear of the future
- Fear of the unknown
- Fear of making decisions
- Fear of dying
- Etc.

SPIRIT OF INSANITY

Luke 8:27 (KJV) "And when he went forth to land, there met him out of the city a certain man, which had devils long time, and ware no clothes, neither abode in any house, but in the tombs"

This spirit is very common among our generation of young people today, it manifests as mental problems, like bipolar, etc.

SPIRIT OF DESPAIR (HEAVINESS)

Isaiah 61:3 "To console those who mourn in Zion, to give them beauty for ashes, the oil of joy for mourning, the garment of praise for the spirit of heaviness; That they may be called trees of righteousness, the planting of the Lord, that He may be glorified."

Heaviness here is the Hebrew word keheh meaning dull, dark, colorless, hopeless, failing, specially a wick burning with very little flame, almost gone out.

SPIRIT OF INFIRMITY

An infirmity is a weakness, disease, or sickness. This spirit is commonly associated with causing sickness and even an unusual fatigue.

Infirmity can be:
- Sickness (Luke 5:15)
- Disease (Luke 8:2)
- Crippling spirit or a physical malfunction (Luke 13:11).

Luke 13:11 (AMP) "And there was a woman there who for eighteen years had had an infirmity caused by a spirit (a demon of sickness). She was bent completely forward and utterly unable to straighten herself up or to look upward."

Matthew 8:16-17 (AMP) 16 "When evening came, they brought to Him many who were under the power of demons, and He drove out the spirits with a word and restored to health all who were sick. 17 And thus He fulfilled what was spoken by the prophet Isaiah, He Himself took [in order to carry away] our weaknesses and infirmities and bore away our diseases."

SPIRIT OF SLUMBER

> Isaiah 29:10 "For the Lord has poured out upon you a spirit of deep sleep, and has closed your eyes (the prophets), and covered your heads (the seers)."

> Romans 11:8 as it is written, "God gave them a spirit of stupor, eyes that would not see and ears that would not hear, down to this very day."

The purpose and goal of this spirit is to:
- Blind people to the Gospel
- Blind them to the Supernatural Power of God.
- Blind them to the Presence of the Holy Spirit.

SPIRIT OF PERVERSION

> Isaiah 19:14 (AMP) "The Lord has mingled a spirit of perverseness, error, and confusion within her; [her leaders] have caused Egypt to stagger in all her doings, as a drunken man staggers in his vomit."

Notice that perversion always leads to error. This word error is the Hebrew word ta'ah, meaning to wander away, to go astray, to become intoxicated. When you are dealing with a spirit of perversion, it can be a sexual perversion, drug addictions, etc.

SPIRIT OF DIVINATION

> Acts 16:16 "As we were going to the place of prayer, we were met by a slave girl who had a spirit of divination and brought her owners much gain by fortune-telling."

This is very common among spirit-filled people. The Amplified version says, *"a slave girl who was pos-*

sessed by a spirit of divination [claiming to foretell future events and to discover hidden knowledge]." People operating under the spirit of divination claim things. It puffs up and does not bear the Heart of the Father. It's about self and not the Kingdom.

The word divination is the Greek word "python." Its goal is to stifle, constrict, and limit true prophetic ministry.

A FAMILIAR SPIRIT

This spirit is one that is familiar with family details, information, generational iniquities. This spirit tries to deceive family members through sickness, symptoms, even at times after family members are dead, through speaking to the dead, which is strictly forbidden by God (Deuteronomy 18:10).

Familiar spirits will also try to attack you, with past issues you have overcome, if it's emotional in nature it will try to cause you to identify again with those emotions and open doors. If it's sickness, it will do the same.

> 1 Samuel 28:7-8 (KJV) "Then said Saul unto his servants, 'Seek me a woman that hath a familiar spirit, that I may go to her, and inquire of her.' And his servants said to him, 'Behold, there is a woman that hath a familiar spirit at Endor.' And Saul disguised himself, and put on other raiment, and he went, and two men with him, and they came to the woman by night: and he said, 'I pray thee, divine unto me by the familiar spirit, and bring me him up, whom I shall name unto thee.'"

(See also Deuteronomy 18:11, 2 Kings 23:24, Isaiah 8:9)

SPIRIT OF WHOREDOMS

This includes adultery, fornication, prostitution and idolatry. Homosexuality is also the working of this spirit. You can see this spirit operating as people are drawn into all sorts of sexual sins, flirting, inappropriate worldly dress, sexual sensuality, and body movements.

> Hosea 4:12 "My people inquire of a piece of wood, and their walking staff gives them oracles. For a spirit of whoredom has led them astray, and they have left their God to play the whore."

In my experience, when doing deliverance from this spirit, people will manifest very sensual movements.

SPIRIT OF PRIDE

It's an excessively high opinion of oneself or one's accomplishments. To be haughty means to be lifted up.

> Proverbs 16:18-19 "Pride goeth before destruction, and a haughty spirit before a fall. Better it is to be of a humble spirit with the lowly, than to divide the spoil with the proud".

LYING

> "Now therefore, behold, the LORD hath put a lying spirit in the mouth of these thy prophets, and the LORD hath spoken evil against thee" (2 Chronicles 18:22). (See also 1 Kings 22:21-23; 1 John 4:6)

ANTICHRIST SPIRIT

The word Christ means the anointed one. An antichrist spirit is just that—antichrist or anti-anointing. This also means he is anti- Christians or anti-you. This spirit is set against Christ and the Holy Spirit.

1 John 3:3 (ESV) "and every spirit that does not confess Jesus is not from God. This is the spirit of the antichrist, which you heard was coming and now is in the world already.

"Little children, it is the last time: and as ye have heard that antichrist shall come, even now are there many antichrists; whereby we know that it is the last time" (1 John 2:18 KJV).

UNCLEAN SPIRIT

This spirit can manifest by:
1. Impure thought life.
2. Torment of the mind.
3. Shame, Condemnation
(Mark 5:8) that is continually tormented with perverse thinking. It can also speak of an unclean spirit in a territory (Zechariah 13:2).

"For he said unto him, Come out of the man, thou unclean spirit" (Mark 5:8).

DEAF & DUMB SPIRIT

This spirit manifests through infirmity, especially speech impediments, but can also manifest in a spiritual way. In the following scripture, Jesus speaks to this spirit.

Mark 9:17-27 "And someone from the crowd answered him, 'Teacher, I brought my son to you, for he has a spirit that makes him mute. 18 And whenever it seizes him, it throws him down, and he foams and grinds his teeth and becomes rigid. So I asked your disciples to cast it out, and they were not able.' 19 And he answered them, 'O faithless generation, how long am I to be with you? How long am I to bear with you? Bring him to me.' 20 And they brought the boy to him. And when the spirit saw him, immediately it convulsed the boy, and he fell on the ground and rolled about, foaming at the mouth. 21 And Jesus asked his father, 'How long has this been happening to him?' And he said, 'From childhood. 22 And it has often cast him into fire and into water, to destroy him. But if you can do anything, have compassion on us and help us.' 23 And Jesus said to him, "If you can! All things are possible for one who believes.' 24 Immediately the father of the child cried out and said, 'I believe; help my unbelief!' 25 And when Jesus saw that a crowd came running together, he rebuked the unclean spirit, saying to it, 'You mute and deaf spirit, I command you, come out of him and never enter him again.' 26 And after crying out and convulsing him terribly, it came out, and the boy was like a corpse, so that most of them said, 'He is dead.' 27 But Jesus took him by the hand and lifted him up, and he arose.

SPIRIT OF DECEPTION

Some spirits mislead or deceive one into error and corruption. This spirit will first try to separate or cause you to depart.

1 Timothy 4:1"Now the Spirit expressly says that in later times some will depart from the faith by devoting themselves to deceitful spirits and teachings of demons,"

SPIRIT OF ERROR

The spirit of error is the Greek word plane, this spirit leads one astray from the right path. Error believes what is untrue, incorrect and wrong. It is a distortion of truth, a perversion and twist of it and from it.

> "We are from God. Whoever knows God listens to us; whoever is not from God does not listen to us. By this we know the Spirit of truth and the spirit of error." (1 John 4:6).

SPIRIT OF THE WORLD

This is very prevalent in our generation. It's nothing new; but its goal is to draw people to worldly standards and its culture.

> "Now we have received not the spirit of the world, but the Spirit who is from God, that we might understand the things freely given us by God." (1 Corinthians 2:12 Italics added).

SPIRIT OF TREACHERY

Those operating by this spirit are disloyal, give a false appearance of safety or reliability and will sell you out. The result is a breach of trust, breaking covenant, and betraying commitment.

Abimelech had killed Gideon's 70 sons to gain rulership. Because of this dishonor to Gideon, God sent a spirit to stir trouble and deal treacherously with him.

> "Then God sent an evil spirit between Abimelech and the men of Shechem; and the men of Shechem dealt treacherously with Abimelech" (Judges 9:23).

SPIRIT OF MURDER

"And Saul hurled the spear, for he thought, 'I will pin David to the wall.' But David evaded him twice." (1 Samuel 18:11)

"Then a harmful spirit from the Lord came upon Saul, as he sat in his house with his spear in his hand. And David was playing the lyre. And Saul sought to pin David to the wall with the spear, but he eluded Saul so that he struck the spear into the wall. And David fled and escaped that night. Saul sent messengers to David's house to watch him, that he might kill him in the morning. But Michal, David's wife, told him, 'If you do not escape with your life tonight, tomorrow you will be killed.'" (1 Samuel 19:9-11).

COMMON CAUSES OF CURSES

Proverbs 26:2 "Like a sparrow in its flitting, like a swallow in its flying, a curse that is causeless does not alight."

Curses have a reason or legal ground to manifest in the lives of people. Curses are a result of sin or someone in the family rebelling against God.

- Shedding Innocent Blood – Genesis 4:9-11 – Cain was cursed because he killed Abel.
- Sexual Perversion – Genesis 9:20-25 – Canaan, the grandson of Noah, was cursed because of his father's sexual perversion. It says that Ham saw Noah naked, and because of that Canaan was cursed.

Romans 1:21-32 21 "because, although they knew God, they did not glorify Him as God, nor were thankful, but became futile in their thoughts, and their foolish hearts were darkened. 22 Professing to be wise, they became fools, 23 and changed the glory of the incorruptible God into an image made like corruptible man—and birds and four-footed animals and creeping things.24 Therefore God also gave them up to uncleanness, in the lusts of their hearts, to dishonor their bodies among themselves, 25 who exchanged the truth of God for the lie, and worshiped and served the creature rather than the Creator, who is blessed forever. Amen.26 For this reason God gave them up to vile passions. For even their women exchanged the natural use for what is against nature. 27 Likewise also the men, leaving the natural use of the woman, burned in their lust for one another, men with men committing what is shameful, and receiving in themselves the penalty of their error which was due.28 And even as they did not like to retain God in their knowledge, God gave them over to a debased mind, to do those things which are not fitting; 29 being filled with all unrighteousness, sexual immorality, wickedness, covetousness, maliciousness; full of envy, murder, strife, deceit, evil-mindedness; they are whisperers, 30 backbiters, haters of God, violent, proud, boasters, inventors of evil things, disobedient to parents, 31 undiscerning, untrustworthy, unloving, unforgiving, unmerciful; 32 who, knowing the righteous judgment of God, that those who practice such things are deserving of death, not only do the same but also approve of those who practice them."

1. Idols and Abominations

Deuteronomy 7:25-26 – Bringing idols and abominations into your house will bring curses. Some of today's idols are: pornography, drugs, perverse objects, paintings, art, books, music, etc...occult items.

2. Old Sins

Joshua 6:26 – says "Cursed be the man before the Lord, that raises up and builds this city Jericho..." Many have been forgiven of past sins and received freedom. Cursed is the man that rebuilds those things and reintroduces it into the lives of people. For example: ungodly soul ties and curses that were destroyed by the power of God, addictions and sexual perversions, or spiritualism and witchcraft. To reintroduce such things into people's lives after they have been free brings a curse.

3. Jezebel Spirit

2 Kings 9:30-34 – says that Jezebel was a "cursed woman." This spirit, is controlling, manipulating, seducing, and power hungry, it makes people spiritual eunuchs.

4. The Spirit of Pride

Psalm 119:21 – "Thou hast rebuked the proud that are cursed, which do err from thy commandments."

5. Trusting man, not God

Jeremiah 17:5-6 says "cursed be the man that trusts in man, and makes flesh his arm, and whose heart departs from the Lord."

6. Following False Ministers and Ministries

Jeremiah 48:10 – "Cursed be the one that does the work of the Lord deceitfully..."

7. Corrupted Sacrifices

Malachi 1:14 - (NLT) "Cursed is the cheat who promises to give a fine ram from his flock but then sacrifices a defective one to the Lord. For I am a great king," says the Lord of Heaven's Armies, "and my name is feared among the nations!"

8. Not giving God all the Glory and Honor

Malachi 2:1-2 - "Listen, you priests—this command is for you! 2 Listen to me and make up your minds to honor my name," says the Lord of Heaven's Armies, "or I will bring a terrible curse against you. I will curse even the blessings you receive. Indeed, I have already cursed them, because you have not taken my warning to heart."

9. Not Tithing

Malachi 3:8-10 - 8 Will man rob God? Yet you are robbing me. But you say, 'How have we robbed you?' In your tithes and contributions.9 You are cursed with a curse, for you are robbing me, the whole nation of you. 10 Bring the full tithe into the storehouse, that there may be food in my house. And thereby put me to the test, says the Lord of hosts, if I will not open the windows of heaven for you and pour down for you a blessing until there is no more need." Matthew 23:23 "Woe to you, scribes and Pharisees, hypocrites! For you tithe mint and dill and cumin, and have neglected the weightier matters of the law: justice and mercy and faithfulness. These you ought to have done, without neglecting the others.)"

10. Soulish Talk and Prayers

James 3:14-15 says, "7 People can tame all kinds of animals, birds, reptiles, and fish, 8 but no one can tame the tongue. It is restless and evil, full of deadly poison. 9 Sometimes it praises our Lord and Father, and sometimes it curses those who have been made in the image of God. 10 And so blessing and cursing come pouring out of the same mouth. Surely, my brothers and sisters, this is not right! 11 Does a spring of water bubble out with both fresh water and bitter water? 12 Does a fig tree produce olives, or a grapevine produce figs? No, and you can't draw fresh water from a salty spring. 13 If you are wise and understand God's ways, prove it by living an honorable life, doing good works with the humility that comes from wisdom. 14 But if you are bitterly jealous and there is selfish ambition in your heart, don't cover up the truth with boasting and lying. 15 For jealousy and selfishness are not God's kind of wisdom. Such things are earthly, unspiritual, and demonic. 16 For wherever there is jealousy and selfish ambition, there you will find disorder and evil of every kind. 17 But the wisdom from above is first of all pure. It is also peace loving, gentle at all times, and willing to yield to others. It is full of mercy and good deeds. It shows no favoritism and is always sincere."

- Proverbs says that the power of life and death are in the tongue.
- We must not gossip, slander, accuse with our mouth.
- We must not do accusatory and condemnatory prayers.
- Dominating or manipulative prayers.

APPENDIX C

6 KEYS TO EFFECTIVE DELIVERANCE MINISTRY

The ministry of deliverance is vital and critical in the hour we live in. More than ever, we face a prevailing doctrine that instills in people their dependence in self and not the power of God to be free from oppressive works of Satan.

I believe more than ever believers need to step into a realm of supernatural dependency on the Holy Spirit to exercise their authority to destroy the works of the devil. We will not win the conflict at hand in mere human power and reason. It is only through the Spirit of God that we are able to truly set the captives free.

Here are 5 insights that I have seen great effectiveness in understanding and walking out in my own ministry.

THERE IS POWER IN THE NAME OF JESUS

"And these signs shall follow them that believe; In my name shall they cast out devils; they shall speak with new tongues." (Mark 16:17).

"That at the name of Jesus every knee should bow, of things in heaven, and things in earth, and things under the earth" (Philippians 2:10).

We are ambassadors of Christ (2 Corinthians 5:20), we have full authority from Heaven as ambassadors to use the name of Jesus Christ to cast out devils. More than anything, we are sons, when a son calls out to Father God in the name of Jesus Christ, Our Heavenly Father responds.

Let's not be like the sons of Sceva who had heard of the name of Jesus Christ, but had not been with Him. Acts 19:13-16 says

"Then some of the itinerant Jewish exorcists undertook to invoke the name of the Lord Jesus over those who had evil spirits, saying, "I adjure you by the Jesus whom Paul proclaims." Seven sons of a Jewish high priest named Sceva were doing this. But the evil spirit answered them, "Jesus I know, and Paul I recognize, but who are you?" And the man in whom was the evil spirit leaped on them, mastered all of them and overpowered them, so that they fled out of that house naked and wounded."

Devils know and obey those whom have been with Jesus, not those who have heard of Jesus through others. Sooner or later as a believer, you will know that the name in whom you come to set the captives free is the name that set you free from your chains.

BE LED BY THE HOLY SPIRIT

Matthew 12:28 says, "But if it is by the Spirit of God that I cast out demons, then the kingdom of God has come upon you."

First you must have a relationship with the Holy Spirit; He is the one that will guide you into the powerful truth of freedom. Many attempt to do deliverance on head knowledge, when demons can never be talked out, negotiated out, or manipulated out. You cannot make deals with demons. They have a mandate of destruction and must they must be cast out. The Holy Spirit brings this revelation at the moment of conflict, with empowering grace in the name of Jesus Christ.

The Greek word for cast out is ekballo, meaning to...Violently drive out Expel by force. Command to depart.

PLEAD THE BLOOD OF JESUS

Revelation 12:11 says "And they have conquered him by the blood of the Lamb and by the word of their testimony, for they loved not their lives even unto death."

The Blood of Jesus Christ is a powerful living testament of redemption and salvation for us and eternal judgment to them (DEMONS). They tremble at the mention of His Powerful Name and the blood.

LEARN TO MINISTER THE ANOINTING ON YOUR LIFE

Isaiah 10:27 says,

"And it shall come to pass in that day, that his burden shall be taken away from off thy shoulder, and his yoke from off thy neck, and the yoke shall be destroyed because of the anointing."

Isaiah 61:1 "The Spirit of the Lord God is upon me, because the Lord has anointed me to bring good news to the poor; he has sent me to bind up the brokenhearted, to proclaim liberty to the captives, and the opening of the prison to those who are bound;"

God anoints believers for the work of the ministry. We must learn to minister that anointing. One of the reasons people lose their anointing is because they do not use it. They do not exercise it. God continues to pour it out upon those who use it to set the captives free.

TRAVAILING PRAYER

Romans 8 says,

"22 For we know that the whole creation has been groaning together in the pains of childbirth until now. 23 And not only the creation, but we ourselves, who have the first fruits of the Spirit, groan inwardly as we wait eagerly for adoption as sons, the redemption of our bodies. 24 For in this hope we were saved. Now hope that is seen is not hope. For who hopes for what he sees? 25 But if we hope for what we do not see, we wait for it with patience.26 Likewise the Spirit helps us in our weakness. For we do not know what to pray for as we ought, but the Spirit himself intercedes for us with groanings too deep for words. 27 And he who searches hearts knows what is the mind of the Spirit, because the Spirit intercedes for the saints according to the will of God."

Exodus 2:23-25,

"says During those many days the king of Egypt died, and the people of Israel groaned because of their slavery and cried out for help. Their cry for rescue from slavery came up to God. 24 And God heard their groaning, and God remembered his covenant with Abraham, with Isaac, and with Jacob. 25 God saw the people of Israel—and God knew."

I find myself often in travailing prayer before I minister corporate deliverance or even individual deliverance. There is a powerful transaction that happens in the Spiritual Realm. When we enter into travailing prayer, it destroys the chains of Satan, and it sets captives free. I have found myself, reminded by the Holy Spirit during ministry, saying "This is why you travailed earlier!" I did not understand it at that moment, until the appointed time.

FASTING & PRAYER

Mark 9:14-29 | Matthew 17:14-20 | Luke 9:37-43

We find the story of the father who brought his son to Jesus's disciples for deliverance. When the disciples tried to cast out the demon, they were unable to do so. As Jesus walks towards them, He notices the commotion and realizes that the Scribes are debating with His disciples. Jesus asks what they are debating about.

After the father explains his situation, Jesus gives them an interesting answer: "He answered, "O faithless generation, how long shall I be with you? How long shall I bear with you? Bring him to Me."" (Mark 9:19, MEV)

His answer had always puzzled me. He rebukes them for being a faithless generation. Or a generation that lacks trust and faith. Later Jesus affirms the need for faith again: *"Jesus said, "If you can believe, all things are possible to him who believes."* (Mark 9:23, MEV)

The response of the child's father is also very revealing *"Immediately the father of the child cried out with tears, 'Lord, I believe. Help my unbelief!'"* (Mark 9:24, MEV). The disciples privately asked Jesus later why they could not cast out the demon. The Gospel according to Luke does not address this issue, while Mark and Matthew do. In Mark 9:29 Jesus says: "He said to them, *'This kind cannot come out except by prayer and fasting.'"* (Mark 9:29, MEV)

The reason I found these answers interesting is that Jesus specifically addresses why they were not able to cast out the demon. One of the classes I took in ministry training college was on how to study your bible. I remember my teacher would always say *"Context, context, context!"* He would say that to determine the context of what Jesus was saying accurately; you had to not only to read the verse, but the chapter, then the whole gospel and then use the whole counsel of the Word of God.

From this advice, we can see that each writer of the gospels wanted to include certain details and clue us into what they were perceiving and what was being revealed to them through Jesus. While Mark says that the reason the disciples could not cast out the demon was ultimately prayer and fasting. Matthew goes into more detail and affirms that faith is the ultimate reason why: *"Then the disciples came to Jesus privately and said, "Why could we not cast it out?" He said to them, "Because of your little faith. For truly, I say to you, if you have faith like a grain of mustard seed, you will say to this mountain, 'Move from here to there,' and it will move, and nothing will be impossible for you.""* (Matthew 17:19–20, ESV)

Prayer and fasting are powerful ways we can grow in our faith. We can see clearly through reading the context of this story that Jesus was ultimately addressing an internal lack of faith in the disciples and the means to change this lack was through prayer and fasting. Many people say that *"this kind"* refers to the demonic spirit. But I believe, that "this kind" is referring to *"unbelief."* While prayer and fasting can help in deterring demonic spirits in our life, it is prayer and fasting that gives us access to faith to believe that we can cast out demonic intruders in our life and the life of others.

In conclusion, I encourage you not only to pray and fast so that you can stay strong in your spiritual walk with God; utilize prayer and fasting to access the mighty power of faith that can evict any intruders in your life and the life of others.

PRACTICAL WISDOM & INSTRUCTIONS FOR DELIVERANCE MINISTRY

INSTRUCTIONS

The word spirit is the word pneuma, meaning breath. Demonic spirits are associated with breath. When we command a demon to go, don't worry about manifestations or anything, we command it to go and take a breath and exhale. We have people around that will come pray for you in case anything happens. Don't pray in tongues, don't pray in English, just breath out and let God deliver you!

I. Prayer of Repentance from Sin - Repentance is a decision to turn away from sin and to recognize you need to forgiveness for missing the mark.

2. Prayer to Renounce Sin and Generational Curses - Renunciation is to give up and put aside voluntarily. It is a formal statement of giving something up.

3. Prayer of Forgiveness - Forgiveness is choosing to cancel someone's offense against you, letting go of your anger or judgment against them without expecting them to do or say anything to you.

DEMON GROUPINGS:

This list is to help you identify how demons can work by their roots and their fruit. It's important to know and believe that once the demonic has been cast out, you must dismantle any wrong belief system, introduce the truth of Christ, and have faith in His power to finish and perfect His work in us.

- **BITTERNESS** - RESENTMENT, HATRED, UN-FORGIVINESS, ANGER, MURDER
- **REBELLION** - SELF-WILL, STUBBORNNESS, DISOBEDIENCE,ANTI-SUBMISSIVENESS, ABSALOM.
- **STRIFE** - BICKERING, ARGUMENT, FIGHTING.
- **CONTROL** - WITCHCRAFT, MANIPULATION.
- **REJECTION** - FEAR OF REJECTION AND SELF-REJECTION.
- **INSECURITY** - INFERIORITY, SELF-PITY, LONELINESS, SHYNESS, INADEQUACY, FEAR.

- **JEALOUSY** - ENVY, DISTRUST.
- ESCAPE - PASSIVITY, SLEEPINESS, ALCO-HOL, DRUGS, ADDICTIONS.
- **DEPRESSION** - DESPAIR, DISCOURAGE-MENT, HOPELESSNESS, SUICIDE, DEATH, INSOMNIA.
- **CURSING** - COURSE JESTING, GOSSIP, CRITICISM, BACKBITING, MOCKERY, BELITTLING.
- **COMPULSIVE/ADDICTIVE** - DRUGS, COCAINE, ALCOHOL, MEDICA-TIONS, CUTTING,PORNOGRAPHY, MASTURBATION.
- **SELF-ACCUSATION**-SELF-HATRED, SELF-CONDEMNATION.
- **GUILT** - CONDEMNATION, SHAME, UN-WORTHINESS, EMBARRASMENT.
- **SEXUAL IMPURITY** - LUST, FANTASY, MASTURBATION, INCEST, RAPE, FORNICA-TION, HOMOSEXUALITY, LESBIANISM.
- **UNBELIEF** - DOUBT, DEAF AND DUMB SPIRIT.
- **INFIRMITY** - ASTHMA, DIABETES, MI-GRAINE HEADACHES, TUMORS, CANCERS, HEART PROBLEMS.

DISCERNING BETWEEN THE FLESH VS. DEMONIC INFLUENCE

I mentioned earlier that one of the dangers of overemphasizing in spiritual warfare and deliverance is that everything gets attributed to demonic influence. Thankfully, the Holy Spirit inspired the writers of Scripture to reveal to us not only the realm of the spirit but also the works of the natural realm.

In Galatians, the Apostle Paul clearly describes the works of the flesh in our mortal bodies. We should not ignore the fact that any of these works of the flesh can give access to demonic intrusion in our life, often reinforcing cycles of bondage. When we try to be free from them, the enemy can use them to torment and destroy our life.

"I say then, walk in the Spirit, and you shall not fulfill the lust of the flesh. For the flesh lusts against the Spirit, and the Spirit against the flesh. These are in opposition to one another, so that you may not do the things that you please. But if you are led by the Spirit, you are not under the law. Now the works of the flesh are revealed, which are these: adultery, sexual immorality, impurity, lewdness, idolatry, sorcery, hatred, strife, jealousy, rage, selfishness, dissensions, heresies, envy, murders, drunkenness, carousing, and the like. I warn you, as I previously warned you, that those who do such things shall not inherit the kingdom of God." (Galatians 5:16–21, MEV)

As a general guideline, if a person has dealt with a continuous pattern of sin in their life, a demonic influence has already reinforced it as a bondage in their life. This individual would need deliverance to begin the process of restoration but also will need to deal with the mindsets and habits of sin they have developed. One easy way to see if demonic spirits were influencing the person is how they feel after being delivered, for example, if the individual senses a measure of freedom, but not complete freedom. Two things are important to complete the process:

RENEW YOUR MIND

Often, the greatest battle will take place in the mind. Scripture declares to us that we have the mind of Christ. (1 Cor. 2:16)

DEVELOP THE FRUIT OF THE SPIRIT

Galatians gives us the antidote to the works of the flesh. It is a pursuit of developing the fruit of the Spirit of God in our life.

"But the fruit of the Spirit is love, joy, peace, patience, gentleness, goodness, faith, meekness, and self-control; against such there is no law." (Galatians 5:22– 23, MEV)

ABOUT THE AUTHOR

Edgar for over 10 years has be a part of Christian International Ministries Network founded by Bishop Bill Hamon the Father of the Prophetic Movement. His training and upbringing has come through personal mentoring under the House of the Prophets. He is part of the ministry staff, an instructor in the Apostolic Prophetic Trainings (APT) and Vision Leadership Institute. Under the leading of the Holy Spirit, he flows under a Prophetic-Apostolic Teaching mantle that brings reformation to the lives of believers and transforming their hearts to be passionate seekers of God's will and purpose for their life.

He along with his wife, Victoria, are coordinators of Christian International en Español, they are Associate Ordained Ministers of Vision Church @ Christian International under Apostles Tom and Jane Hamon. They travel nationally and internationally reaching souls, families and nations for Christ. In May of 2016 they joined the Pastoral Team of Vision Church Fort Walton Beach under Pastor's Ned and Laci Maraman. Edgar and Victoria currently reside in Santa Rosa Beach, Fl with their sons, Josiah and David.